The STAR Manager

Donald Cope

Copyright © 2017 Donald Cope

All rights reserved.

ISBN: 978-1977982261
ISBN-10:1977982263

DEDICATION

The STAR Manager is dedicated to the many wonderful managers and mentors I have had the privilege to learn from over the years. It is also dedicated to all who want to make a difference in the world by leading others; to those who have chosen to be stewards of talent and devote themselves to the success of others.

CONTENTS

FOREWARD

CHAPTER

1) THE INVITATION — 1
2) A NEW STAR — 10
3) THE COMPASS — 23
4) THE STAR ANALYSIS — 40
5) PLANNING FOR STARDOM — 52
6) MEETING WITH THE STARS — 69
7) THE NORTH STAR — 83
8) FINDING THE STARS — 99
9) OBSERVING THE STARS — 123
10) COACHING THE STARS — 141
11) ASSESSING THE STARS — 165
12) STAR WORK SESSIONS — 193
13) THE STAR TOOLBOX — 215
14) THE STAR OPPORTUNITY — 231
15) THE STAR NEWS — 245
16) WELCOME TO HONG KONG — 254
17) A NEW BEGINNING — 262

ABOUT THE AUTHOR — 270

FOREWORD

The promotion from individual performer to leading others is one of the most challenging transitions in a person's career. Even when companies have management development processes to prepare a candidate for this transition most new managers find the new assignment to be demanding and at times, overwhelming.

The STAR Manager follows a new manager, Troy Noble, through a journey with a series of mentors. Each mentor helps Troy understand different aspects of management. While the characters are fictional many of the perspectives and teaching points are those taught by real mentors encountered in over 30 years of managing people. These ideas shaped my own management career and serve as tenets to the management training and development programs we design at Shinestar Consulting Services.

At the end of each chapter, I have included "Questions to Consider". These questions will help provide context and relevance throughout the book.

Best wishes as you strive to become a "STAR Manager".

CHAPTER ONE: THE INVITATION

Blessings are often disguised as challenges and problems masquerade as joys.

The sun reflected like a thousand diamonds on the azure blue Caribbean Sea. Troy and Heather lounged together on the deep cushions of the rattan circular daybed on the veranda of their resort bungalow drinking mimosas while gazing on the beautiful morning vista before them.

"It seems like a different world compared to Cleveland, doesn't it?" Troy said quietly.

"It is amazing." Heather answered with a smile, "I'm so glad I'm married to a President's Cup winner. To think you turned around a poorly performing territory to the number one position in the company is remarkable. That you did it in your second year with the company, it's no wonder everyone seems so impressed. How many people won this trip?"

"The trip is supposed to be for the top people in the company. For the sales group that means around ten people. I'm not sure how they measure performance in home office. Still, with Mareno having 200 employees, there are 20 award winners here." Troy answered. "Making the move to Mareno

Bioscience was one of the best decisions I have ever made, besides marrying you, of course. Everything has seemed to come so easily here."

Heather went back into the one-bedroom villa that the company provided for this celebratory trip to change into her swimsuit. Troy continued to stare out at the ocean and daydream about the future.

A couple of minutes later Heather returned still wearing her robe and handed Troy an envelope.

"What's this?' Troy asked.

"I'm not sure. It was slipped under the door with our names on it." She answered.

Troy carefully opened the envelope with the names "Troy and Heather Noble" written in calligraphy and pulled out the folded note card inside. Troy read the message aloud.

"It says, 'Troy and Heather, please join Janay and I at the yacht dock near the main lobby at noon. Please join us for lunch and then go sailing with us this afternoon. Dress casually. Sam Logan'."

"This sounds pretty exciting" Heather said enthusiastically, "Who is Sam Logan?"

"Only the vice president of sales for Mareno Bioscience." Troy said with a smile. "Sam has been a part of Mareno since it was formed nearly ten years ago. People say he's a straight shooter and a strong leader. I think the company is pretty much a reflection of Sam's charisma. I've heard that in the early years there was little more than Sam's vision and dreams for success. He built the original team at Mareno Bioscience and somehow convinced everyone that someday it would be a multi-million-dollar operation. I guess it turned out that he knew what he was talking about. Last year we had sales over $200 million."

"He sounds like an interesting guy." Heather said, "It should be fun to meet him."

"To be honest, I'm a bit nervous." Troy said, "Sam is also known for making snap decisions about people. Everyone says he has a good list and a bad list. Those on the bad list don't last very long. I hope I'm on the good list."

"I'm pretty sure that the number one sales rep in the country is on his good list." Heather said with a laugh.

"I would think, but you never know." Troy answered, "It's a funny thing but people at Mareno seem to either love him or hate him. The people who love him copy his every gesture and expression. You should see it. They mirror him like a monkey in the zoo. Some say Sam saved the company by taking some risks early on. Others who don't like Sam tell a different story. They talk about his arrogance and his failure to consider other's feelings and perspectives."

"Well, maybe we can get to know him today and make up our own minds about him." Heather said, "A man who has achieved so much certainly sounds interesting to me."

"I wouldn't count on much time with Sam today." Troy said, "I imagine all the award winners will be wanting a piece of him. We will likely have a brief conversation. But enough about Sam. Let's go take a walk on the beach this morning before we have to get ready for the sailing event." Troy said.

The beach, like the rest of the resort was pristine. The waves of the ocean gently rolled across the sugar-like sand in clear sheets of salt water that mirrored the rich blue sky. It soon was time to return to the bungalow.

Troy and Heather dressed tastefully for the noon time event. Heather wore a pastel sundress while Troy wore plaid shorts and a polo shirt. When they arrived at the dock they were surprised to find not a large group of award winners but rather a single event coordinator waiting to greet them.

"Ah, Troy and Heather" Eileen, the event coordinator said with a smile. She escorted them to a double-mast Silyon 75-foot schooner at the far end of the dock, a yacht chartered for the day by Mareno Bioscience.

The yacht gleamed with a polished teakwood deck and cloud like sails. Eileen motioned to the couple to come aboard where they were immediately met by a steward holding a tray with glasses of champagne. "Have a great time." Eileen said as she waved goodbye.

Troy and Heather accepted their flutes of champagne in time to hear Sam's booming voice entering the room.

"Welcome aboard." Sam said with a friendly smile. "Troy and Heather let me present my lovely wife, Janay."

Janay, an attractive, blonde, blue-eyed woman at least twenty years the junior of Sam graciously smiled and offered her hand for Troy to shake. She then turned to Heather and gave her a warm hug.

"Janay, why don't you give Heather a tour of the yacht while I show Troy the wheelhouse?" Sam said more as an order than as a request.

"This yacht is so impressive." Troy said looking around at the rich teak and mahogany paneled walls.

"Indeed." Sam answered, "Only the best for one of my rising stars."

"Where are the others?" Troy asked

"Others?" Sam asked confused, "There are no other guests, today. I wanted the opportunity to spend some time with you and for Janay to get to know your lovely wife, Heather."

Troy didn't know what to say.

Sam continued, "I've been paying attention to how you've been managing yourself ever since you came to Mareno. I must say, I've been very impressed by you. You are a hard worker and you get things done. I see you as having great potential. The way you worked through the politics at Cleveland Clinic to get the formulary addition was amazing. Of course, taking a territory from worst to first is quite an accomplishment."

Troy felt as if he was in some wonderful dream. He was dumbfounded by Sam's words.

"Thank you, Sam." Troy managed to say, "I'd have to say that is a great compliment coming from you."

Sam laughed loudly, "You don't have to suck up to me, Troy. You already have the job."

"And I want you to know I appreciate it, too." Troy said, "I love this sales job and really enjoy working for Mareno."

"I'm not talking about the sales job." Sam said, suddenly seeming quite serious. "I'm talking about the southeast manager's position."

Troy was overwhelmed. There were only six sales managers in the company. Surely, Sam couldn't be serious. A manager has twelve to fourteen sales people reporting to them. Troy had never managed anyone except himself.

A wave of panic rushed over Troy making him feel that the blood had been flushed from his body.

"I've never managed people. I don't know if I could even do that job." Troy said.

"Of course, you can do that job." Sam said laughing, "I never make mistakes about who I promote, and I wouldn't be promoting you if you weren't ready."

Troy felt light-headed. On one hand, it was clearly a dream come true. Yet at 29 years old, he had only recently found consistent success as a sales representative. Troy didn't know what a manager's responsibilities were other than what he had observed from his own managers. Troy wondered if he had the skills needed to be a sales manager.

"Look." Sam said, "Here come Heather and Janay. Wait till Heather hears the news."

"What news is that?" Janay asked, as if on cue.

"Well, I've offered Troy the southeast manager's position." Sam said putting his arm around Troy's shoulder. "Now, all he has to do is have the good sense to accept."

Heather looked confused, then broke into a smile. "Really? I'm proud of you Troy."

Janay looked at Troy and asked him point blank, "So you *are* going to accept, aren't you?"

'Well, I'm honored, of course." Troy said, "But wouldn't this require a move? Heather has a career too. I mean, there's the financial picture and understanding the expectations of a manager's position. We would have a lot to think about."

Heather surprised Troy by saying, "I'm sure we could work through the details."

Janay laughed, "See, there may be less to think about than you thought."

"Troy, all the details will work out. The relocation, the financial situation, expectations. I've got you covered. Let me ask you something, Troy." Sam asked looking straight into his eyes. "Do you trust me? Do you trust that I know how to lead this company forward?"

Troy seemed almost hypnotized and completely overcome by Sam's charisma.

"Yes." Troy answered without hesitation.

"Then trust me with your career." Sam answered,

Troy looked over at Heather who seemed to be encouraging his response.

"Okay, Sam." Troy said with genuine admiration and yet still deep concern. "Okay, I'll take the job"

"Congratulations!" Sam shouted. Janay, Heather, Sam and the entire crew of the schooner broke out in applause.

The afternoon was perfect. Not a cloud in the Caribbean sky and the water as smooth as ice. Janay and Heather became fast friends while Sam discussed with Troy the details of his quite comfortable salary. Troy was humbled to know he would also be granted stock options and benefits.

That evening when Troy returned to the hotel he immediately called his current manager and mentor, Linh Ng. She answered on the first ring.

"I've been waiting to hear the news," she said, "Did you accept the job?'

"Linh, I didn't even know I was being considered for management. This came as a complete shock." Troy answered.

"Troy, you are the best hire I've ever made. From your very first day on the job, I had a feeling that you would be a real star. I've never seen anyone make the transition so quickly and effectively. Sam and I have talked about you for months." Linh said.

"But you never told me." Troy said, "I mean you've worked with me so much over these two years and you've stretched me in ways I had never experienced but I didn't know you were thinking about me for a manager's position."

"Well, of course." Linh said, "Good managers are constantly looking for promotable talent and they have the responsibility to help develop it."

"Thank you, Linh." Troy said, "You have been a really good manager. You know I will need to call on you often in the new job."

"Ah, so you did accept." Linh said with satisfaction, "I am so excited for you."

The conversation continued with Linh providing some advice and continuing her accolades. Troy's mind kept wandering. He was excited yet anxious about this new opportunity. As the conversation ended Troy became quiet as he looked out over the starlit ocean.

Troy's anxiety deepened…he knew nothing of being a manager and he was terrified of what awaited him in his new role.

QUESTIONS TO CONSIDER

1) Were you fully prepared to become a manager?

2) What level of responsibility does a company have to prepare candidates for management?

3) How do you prepare yourself for greater responsibility?

CHAPTER TWO: THE NEW STAR

The official announcement of Troy's promotion wasn't to be made until mid-week, but Troy's life changed immediately. Sam's executive assistant, Deirdre arranged for Troy to travel directly back to the company headquarters in Boston while Heather returned to Cleveland.

Heather worked as a shift nurse at a 120-bed community hospital near the suburb where they lived. The idea of a move away from Cleveland was exciting to Heather even though it would be the first time that she would be far away from her parents.

Troy's new position would necessitate a move to Atlanta where the southeast region office resides. Heather soon learned that management at Mareno expected her to begin the process of preparing for the house-hunting trip on her own, even though she was expected back at work the following day. This seemed an unfair burden as if the company believed she didn't have a life of her own.

"It will be crazy for a while." Troy told Heather as they waited for her plane to depart at the airport. "Sam, wants us to move as quickly as possible. I know this will put extra stress on both of us. But, don't worry. It will settle down in time."

"I'm really proud of you." Heather answered, "I realize this was a surprise and that we will both have to make some sacrifices. I really don't mind leaving my job behind. It has been stressful for a while, now. Still, I'll have to give proper notice."

"You know, Heather you made more money than I did when we first got together. You carried us in those early days." Troy said, "With the kind of raise I got with this job you probably wouldn't even have to work if you didn't want to."

"I can't sit at home and be your trophy wife." Heather said with a smile, "I will still want to work. Still, I'm comfortable following your career for a while. Maybe, I will go back to school and get my masters degree. It would be nice to have a higher-level position in nursing."

"That sounds exciting." Troy said, "I think you'll have a lot of options in Atlanta. In the meantime, don't be too stressed about the move. Everything will move pretty quickly but we will work through it together."

Heather smiled, "I know. I'll start preparing when I get home."

The gate agent called for boarding. Troy kissed Heather tenderly before walking to his own flight in the adjacent terminal.

"Have a safe flight." Troy whispered, "I love you."

As soon as Troy arrived in Boston he knew that the craziness he had told Heather was temporary would last for more than "just a little while". The Vice President of Finance, Sarah Shepherd was returning from the President's Cup event on the same plane as Troy and offered to drive him to his hotel near the office. Sarah told Troy she had several burning issues she wanted to address.

"There are a few things you'll need to handle right away." Sarah told Troy as she drove. "The southeast team has been behind forecast for quite a while. In fact, of the six sales teams, the southeast is lagging far behind in sixth place. Furthermore, if the company doesn't achieve its forecast, it will likely be because of the southeast. You have a lot on your shoulders."

"Why do you think they're performing poorly?" Troy asked.

"Sam thinks it's been poor leadership and I think he's right but there's so much more to it than that. I think there are some bad apples in the basket down there. You'll probably have to do some housecleaning. Not only that, but I think there's some funny business going on regarding expenses."

"Really?" Troy asked.

"I'm not sure yet." Sarah answered, "But I'm having an expense audit done as we speak, and I won't be surprised if we find that there are multiple violations."

"I see." Troy said contemplating the difficulties that were awaiting him.

"Oh yeah." Sarah added, "And I don't want to pile things on, but believe it or not, you will have to submit your business plan for next year within the next month.

"No worries." Troy answered, although he had plenty. Troy hadn't ever completed a true business plan and wasn't sure he knew what was required.

"Do you think you could send me an example of a business plan that is really top notch?" Troy asked.

The STAR Manager

"Sure." Sarah answered. "I'll send you Jim Martin's from the Western Region. He's an ace at business planning. By the way, I want you to know that I'm here for you. You have a big job down there in the southeast. I really wish you the best."

Sarah dropped Troy at the front entrance of the Marriott and told him that she would see him at the office.

Troy checked in and unpacked his laptop even before opening his suitcase. As soon as Troy opened his company email he could see that the previous southeast region manager's email had been transferred over. Troy had 123 messages in his mailbox.

At first, Troy tried to read each one. There were messages from sales representatives, customers and from various departments within home office. There were also messages from Sam; some addressed only to Troy while others were addressed to the regional managers and others still to the entire sales force. There were sales reports with massive EXCEL spreadsheets and detailed graphics. There were reports from human resources regarding recruiting metrics. There were also several messages from the compliance department and two curious messages from Mareno's general counsel.

Troy had read through about 25 messages in his first hour in front of the computer only to find that while he was reading another 9 messages appeared in his "Inbox"

"What have I gotten myself into?" Troy said out loud. He finally closed the computer and got ready for bed. He found it difficult to sleep thinking about all that was ahead.

When Troy arrived at the office at 7am, Deirdre, Sam's executive assistant met him in the lobby.

"Good morning, Troy." she said enthusiastically, "Are you ready for the madhouse?"

"Definitely." Troy said with more confidence than he felt.

Troy signed in at the security desk, received his permanent entry pass and then went to the executive suite where Sam had his office. Sam was already at his desk.

"Good morning, Ace." Sam said with a grin. "Let's get a cup of coffee and get started."

Sam led the way down the hall to a small kitchen where the coffee maker was already brewing strong European coffee.

"I love this supercharged coffee." Sam said with a laugh. "There is nothing like bold, Italian coffee to get the day off to a good start."

Troy had barely poured his cup when Sam was already leaving the kitchen walking swiftly back to his office. Troy hurried to catch up.

When they got back to the office Sam told Troy to shut the door behind him and have a seat.

"Okay, this is how things will go down this week." Sam began. "Today we will have a private call with the other regional managers. We'll introduce you as their new colleague. Before the call I've got several appointments set up for you with members of the senior staff. I would suggest you take notes. There's a lot going on right now. Tomorrow, we will announce your promotion to your sales team on a conference call. I don't want you saying a whole lot on that call. Be polite and humble; don't try to set expectations or put out any weird vibes. You'll have plenty of time to get to know the team over the next few weeks.

Then on Wednesday, I want you to go to Atlanta and meet your Administrative Assistant, Carol Kline. She's a peach. You will probably want Heather to join you on Thursday, so you can start looking for a home. If possible, I'd like to see you take care of all that over the weekend. Then do whatever you need to do next week because the following Tuesday begins our national sales meeting here in Boston. You will need to be ready to step up to lead your new team at that time. So...any questions?"

Troy was reeling from Sam's rapid-fire communication. "I'm sure I'll have many questions but for now, I think I'm good." Troy answered.

"Great." Sam said, "Check with Deirdre on the way out. She'll give you your appointment schedule. I think our call with the regional managers is at noon. I'll see you back in my office then. By the way Troy, I'm glad to have you on board."

Sam stood up and escorted Troy to the door and out of his office where Deirdre stood waiting.

As Troy greeted Deirdre, Sam went back into his office closing the door behind him.

Deirdre smiled. "I know it's a lot to take in." she said quietly, "but you'll be fine. Sam is kind of full on. His style is like a drive-by shooting. He barks out his instructions and then he's off. You'll get used to it."

Troy took a deep breath and walked to his first appointment. He tried to stay calm and follow Sam's instructions. Each meeting was filled with new information and because Troy was unsure how to differentiate the importance of each topic he tried to write down almost everything.

Monday and Tuesday's meetings went by in a blur and in a flash Troy was back on a plane heading to Atlanta.

Troy was surprised at how exhausting the past few days had been and yet with each day he was invigorated by the challenges he was facing. It was as if he were running on pure adrenaline.

On Wednesday, Troy arrived in Atlanta and immediately drove out to the regional office in Alpharetta. The office was located on the fourth floor of a large, modern office building. Troy took the elevator to the fourth floor and immediately saw the Mareno Bioscience logo on one of the two office suites adjacent to the elevator lobby. Carol Kline was waiting for him as he entered the office suite.

"Impressive, isn't it?" Carol asked, "Welcome to your new office."

Troy was overwhelmed. The office suite was beautifully decorated and spacious with an ample waiting lounge, a reception desk, a conference room and two smaller offices.

Carol walked with Troy to show him around.

"The smaller of the two offices is mine and of course, the larger one is yours" Carol said," As you can see you have a small table with four chairs at one end and a large walnut desk with built-in bookshelves at the other."

From the window, Troy could see the woods and driveway below, as well as a pond off in the distance.

"This is incredible." Troy said. "Carol I'm anxious to get to know you. I've heard many good things."

"All lies, I'm sure." Carol answered with a smile, "Let's go in the conference room. I've laid out files you're going to need and there's a few things I'm sure you'll want to discuss. Remember that I am here to make your life as easy as possible, don't hesitate to ask me for anything you need."

Over the next few hours Troy and Carol went through the various processes and structures that Mareno had in place for management. Carol's knowledge about the sales team and the internal personnel at Mareno's home office was surprising and impressive. Troy knew immediately that the two of them would form a powerful partnership.

After they had discussed the immediate priorities of the southeast region, Carol looked Troy directly eye to eye. "Troy, what scares you the most about your new job?"

"Do I look scared?" Troy asked.

"I've been here almost 9 years." Carol said with a chuckle, "Every new manager looks scared."

"Honestly, Carol." Troy began, "I never saw this coming. I want to do a good job but there is a lot that I don't know. I'm not sure I know what it takes to be a great manager."

"You need a couple of days with Dennis Baker." Carol stated.

"The corporate accounts guy?" Troy asked, "I thought he was put out to pasture. Didn't he manage the midwest region before Linh?"

Carol laughed. "He wasn't put out to pasture. He was one of the best regional managers Mareno ever had. He had a heart attack when he was 59 and asked to take a role that was less stressful; one that would allow him to travel less. Since many of the key hospital systems are in the mid-west the corporate accounts position was a perfect match. Anyway, Dennis could help you make sense of this new role."

When Carol went to lunch Troy picked up the phone and called Sam.

"Sam, Troy here." Troy said.

"Troy, my rising star." Sam answered happily, "How do you like the Atlanta office? It's great, isn't it? And didn't I tell you Carol was terrific? What can I do for you?"

"I was wondering if it would be okay if I went out to Chicago to meet with Dennis Baker. I understand he was a good regional manager and I'd like to see what I might learn from him." Troy asked.

"Troy." Sam answered as if counseling a son, "You are now in charge of a multi-million-dollar region. You don't need my permission to make decisions. I put you in that role because I trust your judgment. Call me when you need help with something major. For everything else, trust yourself as much as I trust you. How's everything going for you so far?"

"Good. No worries." Troy answered.

"Good to hear, Troy. Have a great day." Sam hung up giving Troy a new sense of confidence and a new understanding of what it means to be a regional manager.

Later that day, Heather arrived in Atlanta for the house-hunting trip.

Even though it at first seemed an impossible task to decide on selecting a new home over one long weekend, the company relocation assistant made the process seem flawless. Troy and Heather found a beautiful home only five minutes from the Alpharetta office. Almost as if scripted, they put in an offer and received an acceptance before the end of the weekend.

The house was much larger and more lavish than either Troy or Heather had originally planned but both were carried away by the emotion of owning a luxurious home in a secure gated community. It was certainly a big step up from their 1100 square foot bungalow they rented in Cleveland.

Only a few hours after signing the purchase contract they parted once again at the airport; Heather returning to Cleveland, Troy to Chicago. Dennis had agreed to meet him at the airport.

Troy didn't know what to expect when meeting Dennis. While he was thinking that Dennis was some "has been" manager that had seen better days, he was surprised to see this fit, stylish, dark-haired man who looked more in his forties than early sixties. Dennis was waiting for Troy outside of security when he arrived at Midway airport.

Dennis apparently knew what Troy looked like since he immediately extended his hand with a smile that was ear to ear.

"Troy, welcome to the windy city." Dennis said with a cheery voice. "Glad to finally meet you."

"Likewise." Troy answered. "I've heard some great things about you."

Dennis led Troy through the dated corridors of the Midway terminal toward his car parked in the short-term parking lot.

"Congratulations on the new job." Dennis said enthusiastically.

"Thanks." Troy answered, "But I have to tell you I have a lot of concerns."

"That's a good thing." Dennis laughed. "Many new managers think they have all the answers. It is refreshing to see one that is hungry to learn. One thing I can tell you though is that if Sam thinks you will be a great manager then you probably will be. He has amazing insights towards people."

"I'm not so sure." Troy said, "Didn't he pick my predecessor?"

"Actually, he didn't." Dennis answered, "Brian was selected by the president. Sam did all he could to help the guy but sometimes things don't work out."

Dennis drove Troy over to Panera Bread across from the hotel where Troy would spend the evening.

"Let's go in and get some afternoon coffee." Dennis said with a smile, "After the heart attack I only drink decaf but I still like the taste."

"I heard about that. How is your health now?" Troy asked.

"I feel great!" Dennis answered, "I made some changes in my life that made such a difference. I eat right. I exercise. I also learned how to reduce stress. I've got a feeling we will talk about that later."

The men ordered their coffees and sat down in a booth. Dennis looked across the table and asked, "What is it that you want to know about managing people?"

"Dennis, actually there are many things." Troy started, "I want to really make a difference and I don't want to let Sam down. I mean, I hear you're a bit of an expert. What do you think I need to know?"

"You got a piece a paper?" Dennis asked.

Troy pulled out his briefcase and retrieved a legal pad and a pen.

"Great." Dennis said. "I have something I want you do for me."

"Okay." Troy answered.

"I want you to write down the name of every manager you have ever worked for."

"Everyone? Even those in summer jobs or when I was a kid?" Troy asked.

"Yes." Dennis answered, "Every single one."

Troy took some time with the assignment. He thought all the way back to when he was a busboy at Bob Evans restaurant. He wrote down the name George although he couldn't remember the man's last name. Dennis sat quietly as Troy worked through his list of supervisors. One by one, Troy wrote down names.

"Okay." Troy stated, "I guess that's about it."

"How many names are on your list?"

Troy silently counted the names.

"Ten." Troy said, "That's hard to imagine but I've actually worked for ten different managers, not including Sam, of course."

"Excellent." Dennis answered. "Now I want you to do something else. Go through your list and put a star next to the name of any manager that made a fundamental difference in your life."

Troy looked down at his list. Slowly, he put a star next to three names.

"How many of your managers made a fundamental difference in your life?" Dennis asked.

"Three." Troy answered, "Not including Linh. I mean obviously she has helped me a lot. Still, when you say made a fundamental difference; well that's a pretty small group."

"Interesting, isn't it?" Dennis said, "I'm sure that every single one of those managers wanted to help people. Every single one wanted to make a difference. Yet only three of ten seemed to accomplish that for you. Tomorrow, we're going to talk about why those three were different from the rest. We're going to talk about several concepts that can help a manager get set for success. But more than anything else, we're going to figure out one thing."

"What is that?" Troy asked.

"Troy, I want to help you be a manager that gets a star next to your name for every single one of the people you will have reporting to you. Troy, I want you to be a STAR manager. Tomorrow we're going to figure out how to make that happen."

QUESTIONS TO CONSIDER:

1) What can you learn from Sam's style of leadership? What are the benefits? What are the risks?

2) If you have an administrative assistant, what would be the ideal partnership?

3) Write out the names of every manager you ever worked for:
    a. How many names on the list?
    b. How many of those made a fundamental difference in your life?

4) Would you consider Dennis a leader? What can you learn from his style?

5) How do you adapt to the stress of change?

CHAPTER THREE: THE COMPASS

Dennis had arranged for a meeting room at the hotel where Troy was staying. In the room was a flipchart, markers, a small conference table with a stack of files and plenty of coffee.

Troy was surprised that when he entered the room at 8am, Dennis had already taken up residence.

"Good morning, my friend." Dennis said warmly.

"Good morning." Troy answered, "Sorry, if I'm late."

"You're not late, I'm always early." Dennis said with a laugh, "Get some coffee and let's get started."

Troy inwardly laughed at his earlier thought that Dennis was some "has been". He was clearly as motivated as many of the younger employees and demonstrated a clear sense of urgency.

"What should we cover first?" Troy asked.

"Well, first." Dennis answered, "I have something I want you to read."

Dennis pulled a one-page sheet out of the file that was on the top of the pile handing it to Troy.

Troy looked at the title, "A Tough Day".

"Go ahead and read that article and then we'll talk about it." Dennis directed. Troy began reading.

A Tough Day

Richard Smith, a manager for Martin Products sat down with his wife Sally for breakfast. As she poured Richard a cup of coffee she noticed that he seemed distant.

"What's on your mind, dear?" Sally asked, "You seem really preoccupied this morning."

"Yes." Richard answered, "Today is going to be a tough day."

"Why?" Sally asked, "What's going on?"

"Yesterday my boss called me in to his office. He told me that the company is going through a challenging time and that we're going to have to cut costs."

"Well, companies do that from time to time, don't they?" Sally asked

"Sure, but this time the cuts have to do with personnel." Richard said sadly

"You aren't going to lose your job, are you?" Sally asked in a panic

"No." Richard answered, "But my boss gave me a list of seven employees that I have to lay off. I have to communicate the bad news today."

"That's terrible." Sally answered, "Who do you have to let go?"

"Several people within the sales team; five men and two women." Richard answered

"I can't believe I have to lay off seven people."

"It's actually worse than that Richard," Sally said pensively, "You aren't laying off seven employees; you're laying off seven families."

Richard drank another sip of coffee and shook his head. "Yes, this is really going to be a tough day."

When Troy had finished reading he looked up at Dennis who was watching him.

"What do you think about the article?" Dennis asked.

"It's really sad." Troy answered, "I think the thing I am most uncomfortable with in being a manager is the possibility of firing people. The article is right, that would be a tough day."

"Read it again." Dennis said, "This time don't think about what the manager feels but rather think about the seven people."

Troy read the article again. This time he thought about the five men and two women who were not named in the article but were victims of the cost cutting. He suddenly wondered about their situations. He wondered how old they were, whether they still had children at home, whether they were living paycheck to paycheck.

"Did you see things differently the second time you read it?" Dennis asked.

"Yes." Troy answered, "The first time I was relating to the manager who was going to have a tough day. The second time I thought that his tough day was nothing compared to the day those seven employees were going to have."

"It makes such a difference thinking that way, doesn't it?" Dennis asked, "I love the wife's line about you aren't laying off seven people; you're laying off seven families."

"Yes, that line got me too." Troy said.

"I wanted you to read that because you have been given a much bigger gift than the chance to lead twelve people. In a way, you have been granted stewardship over twelve families. If those twelve people are successful, their families will prosper. If you make life difficult for those employees, their families will be negatively impacted, as well." Dennis said.

"That seems like a lot of responsibility." Troy observed.

"Yes." Dennis answered, "Yet can you think of anything more impactful to do with your life? What a perfect way to make a difference in the world."

"I hope I'm worthy of the job." Troy said quietly, "I am still wondering why Sam chose me for the promotion."

"Sam is a smart guy." Dennis answered, "First, he trusts the judgment of his regional managers and Linh has been a huge advocate for you. She has shown Sam that you are someone who works through the minutia and gets things done; yet someone sensitive to other's feelings. You have a natural humility about you that is disarming. As well, you seem to show good processes for making decisions. Finally, you are getting results; you took your territory from the bottom to the top of the company. I think Sam knows exactly what he's doing."

"Thanks, Dennis." Troy answered with a smile. "I appreciate the vote of confidence."

"Alright then." Dennis said chuckling, "Enough of the love fest. Let's talk a little bit about the STAR manager list that you completed yesterday. I want you to consider the three managers that you gave a "star". What made them special for you?"

"Interesting question." Troy answered. "I actually thought a lot about that last night. I think it was different things from each of them. The first manager with a star was my very first manager when I was fourteen and worked at Bob Evan's as a busboy. I thought he was brash and cold. He tended to order everyone around; not something I would want to emulate."

"Why do you say he made a fundamental difference in your life?" Dennis asked with genuine curiosity.

"He was the first adult who treated me like an adult." Troy answered, "I was only a kid, but George expected me to meet his standards. These were what he called his "non-negotiables". He would get furious if anyone showed up late for work. He expected everyone to act and look professional. Most of all he absolutely demanded that everyone speak to each other in a respectful manner. I was quite aware of these "non-negotiables" and I wanted to live up to them.

"In addition, he had measures of how well each of us did our job. I mean who measures 'busboy effectiveness'? George did. He had two measures; how quickly in seconds it took to clear and clean a table and how many guests per night had to wait for a table to be bussed for them to be seated."

Dennis laughed, "How did you do with that?"

"Quite well." Troy answered with a level of pride that almost embarrassed him. "I could clear and clean a table within twenty seconds. George measured it periodically when the busboys weren't even aware he was in the dining room. Regarding guests having to wait I was the top busboy even though I was the youngest."

"Congratulations." Dennis said with a smile.

"I know. It sounds ridiculous now." Troy said, "But George made a difference in my life because I learned that confidence and pride comes from having clear standards and measures and then performing well against them."

"Did you use what he taught you in other jobs once you progressed after college?" Dennis asked.

"Yes, and even in ordinary day to day life." Troy answered. "I have a workout journal to measure how I'm progressing with fitness. I have financial measures to keep myself on track. At work, even though Mareno doesn't require activity parameters to be monitored I've kept my own log of daily call rate, frequency on key customers and percentage of customers purchasing. I knew I was pretty organized but didn't attribute this to George until I did this exercise."

"Well, you can see how you can apply this to your new position." Dennis stated.

"Absolutely." Troy answered, "I need to carefully think through my standards and expectations but also get the team to think about this. My "non-negotiables" must be clear to the team. If I can lead the team to come up with appropriate metrics, then they will no doubt be able to reach to a higher level of performance."

"Greta Martina in human resources would be able to help with some of this." Dennis noted, "She had been working of performance standards recently and might help you shape your thinking."

"That's a great suggestion." Troy answered as he wrote her name and title in his notepad and typed "Call Greta Martina" in his iPad "To Do" list.

"Who else was a STAR manager for you?" Dennis asked.

"Tim Zokovitz was my sales manager when I got my first real job after college selling radio advertising. Troy said.

"Wow." Dennis said with a whistle, "Tough job."

"You have no idea." Troy said laughing, "Your whole life is a series of rejections with a little bit of success thrown in to keep you hopeful."

"What made Tim great?" Dennis asked.

"I don't know." Troy answered, "It seemed that he really believed in me. He had a way of instilling confidence. He'd always be calling me to see how my customer prospects were coming along, would talk to me about how to move each forward and then excitedly tell me how sure he was that I was going to close each of the deals. When I obtained a signed commitment, I couldn't wait to call him. He always seemed to revel in each of my successes."

"He sounds like a great guy to work for." Dennis observed.

"I would have knocked down a wall for the guy." Troy answered, "Success was addictive. When Tim left the company, I felt like things would never be the same. He invited me to come with him to the new company which was the ultimate vote of confidence. Sadly, Heather and I had started dating and I couldn't relocate. I'll never forget the guy, though."

"What did you take away from your time with Tim?" Dennis asked.

"I learned that each of us is capable of more success than we know. It sometimes takes someone else believing in us to help us see our own potential." Troy answered. "I want to be that kind of manager. I want to inspire each one of my team members."

"I can see that." Dennis answered, "But don't forget that Tim did more than stand on the sidelines and cheer for you. He also followed up regularly with you and helped problem solve each customer situation."

"Thanks for pointing that out." Troy said pensively, "it's funny how I remember the emotion of it all, but you are right Tim always provided a lot of guidance too."

"There's an old quote that I like," Dennis said, "'a person may forget what you say and even what you do but they will never, ever forget the way you make them feel'."

"That's definitely true." Troy replied.

"How about the third STAR manager?" Dennis asked.

"Ah, Claudia Jones, my manager when I was a new hospital representative at Forbes Pharmaceutical." Troy said with a smile.

"Why was she special?" Dennis asked

"Actually, I was scared to death of her." Troy said laughing, "At the time she came into her job I was second to last place in the country of the 30 hospital reps. I thought she was probably coming in to clean house and that I would be the first one to go."

Dennis chuckled, "I bet the first meeting was tough."

"She was amazing." Troy answered, "I remember meeting her at Starbucks. She hadn't even sat down with her coffee before I nervously told her I had never worked so hard in my life and that I was really trying everything I knew to do a good job."

Troy continued, "She smiled warmly and told me that she knew that I was a hard worker and reassured me that my job wasn't in jeopardy. She then told me that we would figure out together how to 'work smart' and get things on track again."

"Was she able to help you figure it out?" Dennis asked.

"Totally." Troy answered, "I simply didn't know how hospitals worked and where sales could be generated. I was working the entire hospital when most prescriptions were written in just one outpatient center. Claudia helped me figure out where to spend my time effectively. The next year I was one of the top representatives in the country."

"What was the big learning you received from Claudia?" Dennis asked.

"She taught me how to analyze my business and then how to make better use of my time and resources. I want to be able to help my team do the same thing although I'm embarrassed to say that I don't really have everything figured out yet with the bioscience market."

"Well, there's obviously a lot to learn in the bioscience arena so it's not surprising that you would still have some gaps in your knowledge. The good news is that you've made good choices thus far in the business."

"Thanks." Troy said quietly.

"People say you have good judgment." Dennis observed

"Thank you." Troy answered

"Do you know what judgment is?" Dennis teased

"Yes." Troy said, "Judgment is when you consistently make good decisions."

Dennis continued to smile broadly ignoring Troy's acknowledgement. "Judgment is the ability to select the best alternative that you see." Dennis defined, "You always select the best alternative that you see."

"Thank you." Troy said tentatively.

"The problem," Dennis continued, "Is that you don't have enough experience. Do you know what experience is?"

"Go on." Troy answered understanding there was a lesson Dennis was trying to provide.

"Experience is how many alternatives you see." Dennis said wisely. He waited for this information to sink in before continuing.

"You see." Dennis continued, "Some managers get three years of experience in one year while others get one-year experience in three. What do you think is the difference between these managers?"

Troy remained in silence trying to unravel the mystery.

"I'm not sure." Troy finally answered.

"The managers that get three years of experience in one are those that ask others for more alternatives." Dennis said proudly as if revealing a sacred truth. "There are many that can help you in this company. The other regional managers, Greta in HR, Sarah in finance, in fact almost anyone is ready and willing to help. You only need to reach out, Troy."

"That's good advice, Dennis." Troy acknowledged, "I guess I've thought of the other regional managers as my competitors."

"That kind of thinking is for lower level positions." Dennis pointed out, "When you are running a region, it is the success of the company that matters more. You should be thinking about how to gain from your peers and how to help them be more successful, as well. While you may at times be under consideration for the same promotions, your ability to work collaboratively with peers is one of the most important attributes for a senior leader."

"That's helpful." Troy said.

"When I was a regional manager and had an issue to work through I always had this formula for problem-solving. First, I would really think through the problem. I often asked my administrative assistant what she thought about the problem. I would make sure I was getting at the root cause rather than a symptom of something deeper." Dennis said

"That makes sense." Troy added.

"Then after I thought I understood the issue," Dennis continued, "I would create three possible ways that I could solve the problem. Once I had crafted these three potential fixes I would then decide which alternative seemed to be the best. Then the phone calls would begin."

"What phone calls?" Troy asked.

"Those to my peers and mentors" Dennis continued, "I would give them a very brief synopsis of the issue, tell them the three alternatives I was considering and the one I was leaning toward. Then I asked a simple question."

"Okay." Troy acknowledged.

"What am I missing?" Dennis said, "I'd always ask what I was missing. This did three things for me. First, it helped me organize my thoughts. Then it allowed me to test my judgment. Third, it gave me more alternatives."

"That makes perfect sense." Troy said enthusiastically.

"That, my friend, is how you can pick up three years' worth of experience in one year."

"That's very helpful, Dennis." Troy said honestly, "I definitely will take these suggestions."

"Wow." Dennis said, "Can you believe our morning is already gone? It's time for lunch. When we get back I want to talk with you about what I call "Life's Pie" and want to talk about the little financial scandal that might be shaping up in the southeast."

"Sounds great." Troy answered as they walked to the pizza buffet at the hotel.

When the two returned from lunch Dennis picked up a marker and approached the flip pad.

"Funny that we ate pizza because I want to talk to you about another kind of pie. This circle represents your life, Troy." Dennis began, "You have at least five slices of your pie."

Dennis segmented the pie chart into five relatively equal portions.

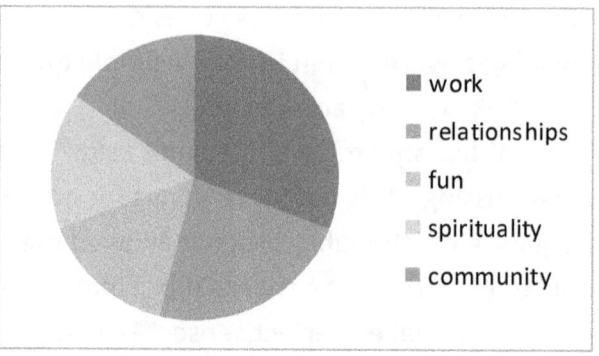

"The slices of your pie are things like work, relationships, community, fun, and spirituality." Dennis said as he labeled each section. "Now, prior to you accepting the promotion how balanced in size were the pieces of your pie?"

"Pretty balanced overall, I'd say" Troy answered.

"Fair enough." Dennis continued, "But since your promotion which piece of the pie has gotten larger?"

Troy laughed, "The work piece, of course."

"Well, since the pie is finite and cannot get bigger," Dennis continued, "For work to get bigger means something else is getting smaller. What piece got smaller?"

"I guess all the pieces have gotten somewhat smaller except work." Troy said thoughtfully. "Community service has pretty much disappeared at this point."

"Okay." Dennis continued, "Suppose next week that you found out that the southeast is under investigation for fraud and embezzlement?"

"Are you kidding me?" Troy said in a panic.

"This is hypothetical." Dennis reassured Troy. "But if that happened what piece of the pie will get larger?"

"Again, it would be work." Troy answered.

"What would get smaller this time?" Dennis continued.

"I hate to say it because it sounds terrible, but probably my spirituality. I'd probably go to church less, compromise on reading, that kind of thing." Troy answered.

"And let's say that Sam called you into his office and said he wanted you to fill in for him while he went on a trip to Europe." Dennis proposed, "Now what?"

"The work slice gets even bigger and I'd probably give up fun." Troy answered as he painfully got the message.

"Here's the sad part." Dennis said, "I've known many managers that started out being superb leaders but then the work eventually overcame them. They first gave up community work, then maybe their spiritual life. They stopped doing fun things when away from work. Sometimes, they even compromised their relationships with their spouse, kids and friends."

"I can see how that happens." Troy observed.

"Well, let me ask you something." Dennis queried, "How much do you want to be around a guy who works all the time, has no interests outside of the company, has no rich spiritual compass and has poor personal relationships?"

"Not much." Troy answered, "I've met people like that and I couldn't even relate to them."

"Exactly." Dennis said enthusiastically, "The real travesty is that those that give up everything for work end up failing at work too. Leadership is about people and people are all about their own Life's Pie. As you said, no one can relate to a guy with a pie with only one slice"

There was brief silence in the room as Dennis let this all sink in. Soon Troy broke the seriousness of the moment and laughed, "Excuse me, I think I better preserve the relationship slice of my pie and go call Heather."

Still serious Dennis answered, "Ferociously protect all the pieces of your pie, Troy. Your happiness and the happiness of those around you depend on it.

"Thanks for sharing this, Dennis." Troy said genuinely, "And I'm not kidding, I want to go call Heather."

When Troy came back after a short phone break Dennis had already moved on to the next topic on his list. On the flipchart in one big word was written "Integrity".

"What's with integrity?" Troy asked defensively, "I think I'm pretty solid in that respect."

"Good." Dennis answered, "Then it should be no problem answering these questions."

Dennis tore the page on the flipchart to reveal the following:

What would you do?
- *If you found that an employee stole food from the cafeteria to feed her children?*
- *Your second largest customer said they would cancel all their orders unless you fire their sales representative?*
- *A highly-regarded opinion-leader told you they would endorse your product if you would include them in the international speaker's bureau?*
- *A sales representative was in last place in the company two years in a row while his daughter was being treated for a childhood cancer.*

"I totally get what you're saying, Dennis." Troy said, "I know these are all tough dilemmas. I think what I would do is what we talked about earlier regarding problem solving. I'd define the problem, think of alternatives, identify the one I was leaning toward and then ask others for their thoughts."

"That's a good approach, as we talked about." Dennis answered, "But there's something else at play in each of these issues. These issues all involve integrity. You remember how you talked about George having clear standards? As a manager, you have to think through not only work standards but your own personal morals; your own compass of right and wrong."

"Yes. I think that's true." Troy agreed.

"Integrity is alignment between your beliefs and actions." Dennis said, "I learned early in my career that I would allow someone to criticize my judgment but that I would never put myself in a situation where others could question my integrity."

"That's a powerful and sobering thought." Troy said

"Yes." Dennis answered, "And from what I hear about the situation you are encountering in the southeast region, one that you may need to draw from."

"Why do you keep coming back to that?" Troy asked, "Am I getting into a hornet's nest in the southeast?"

"All rumors at this point, Troy." Dennis, "Remember you're not on an island. Anything you need, just ask."

"Thanks for that, Dennis." Troy answered.

Troy glanced at the clock and realized that he had to leave soon to catch his next flight.

"Where are you off to next?" Dennis asked.

"You know that I have to prepare a business plan." Troy said, "I thought it might be a good idea to meet with Jim Martin out in California. Alex, our business analytics specialist is working there this week. I understand that Jim is good at business planning and with Alex helping I should be able to nail down what's going on with the business in the southeast."

"That sounds like an excellent plan." Dennis reinforced.

Troy reached out his hand to shake Dennis's. "Thank you for all you've shared with me." Troy said, "You've taught me a great deal in only a few hours."

"Good luck to you Troy." Dennis answered, "Remember, I'm always here for you."

Troy grabbed his suitcase and headed downstairs to catch the hotel shuttle to the airport. Another amazing day running on nothing but adrenaline.

QUESTIONS TO CONSIDER:

1) What are your "non-negotiable" standards and expectations?

2) What metrics do you use to measure your own performance?

3) How have others instilled confidence in your abilities?

4) How are the slices of your "Life's Pie" distributed?
    a. Are they as you would like them?
    b. If not, what are strategies you can employ to reach the ideal balance?
    c. What obstacles will you experience and how will you overcome them?

5) Who will you include to gain "more alternatives" to difficult problems?

CHAPTER FOUR: THE STAR ANALYSIS

Troy loved traveling to the west coast. The inconvenience of the long plane trip was offset by gaining a few hours making it possible to get much done on the day of arrival. The western region office was in San Diego, one of Troy's favorite cities. Upon landing Troy called Uber and was whisked off to Jim Martin's office in Carlsbad, a few minutes north of the airport.

Jim's administrative assistant greeted Troy upon arrival.

"I'm glad to meet you Troy." Jan said, "Congratulations on your new role."

As Troy shook Jan's hand, suddenly Jim Martin emerged from around the corner. A trim, small-framed man who was meticulously well-groomed and conservatively dressed; Jim defied the laid-back stereotype often representing southern California.

"Welcome Troy." Jim said politely, "Please, come into my conference room. I understand you would like some help with business planning. Of course, I am more than happy to help."

Troy smiled at Jim's "get down to business" approach.

"You are especially in luck this week since Alex is out here working with me." Jim continued. "Alex is invaluable when trying to determine what is achievable for the next year. I don't know how much you know about business analytics but as far as I'm concerned, a guy like Alex is essential."

Troy had little exposure to the business analytics group in the past. Alex was well known throughout the sales group for tracking down missing sales to help sales representatives get credit for their bonus compensation. Alex was also critical whenever the sales territories had to be reorganized during expansion as had occurred nearly every year. What Troy didn't realize is how much Alex helped each regional manager in analyzing the business.

Alex was already in the conference room working in front of two laptops, one of which was attached to a projector. Alex was in his early twenties, dressed in jeans and a white polo shirt. Looking up from the computer, Alex smiled broadly and stood up to shake hands.

"Hi Alex." Troy said, "Pleased to meet you."

"I'm pleased to meet you." Alex answered, "I watched all year as you moved that Cleveland territory from the basement to the top of the company. I hope to go out to the field soon to do my rotation as a sales representative and I'm really anxious to find out your keys to success."

Troy smiled. "I'm not sure what I can teach you. I'm pretty much hoping to learn some things from you."

Jim interrupted, "I'm sure we will all learn from each other. Now Troy, have a seat. We have a lot to cover."

Troy sat down. Jim's style was certainly different. Troy wondered how most people related to him since he was serious and business driven. Still, Troy knew that Jim was the expert on planning and he felt honored to work with him.

"Will the southeast be the top region next year?" Jim asked bluntly.

"I sure hope so." Troy answered.

"Hope is not a strategy." Jim said without emotion. "Everyone hopes. I want to know does the southeast have the capability to be the top region next year?"

Troy hesitated before speaking. "Yes, I think it does."

"You think?" Jim queried, "Whenever I hear someone say they think; I cringe. Leaders don't think. Leaders know. Leaders have fully analyzed their situation and know what's possible. Let me ask you again. Does the southeast have the capability to be the top region next year?"

"I don't know." Troy said with embarrassment.

"Good." Jim answered, "Now we're getting somewhere. For the rest of the day, I want you to work with Alex and the two of you can figure the answer to that question. Alex knows what I'm talking about. Then first thing tomorrow morning, we can begin the process of business planning."

Jim stood up and walked out of the conference room pulling the door shut behind him.

Troy let out his breath. "Wow. That was an interesting conversation."

Alex laughed. "That's Jim." he said, "He's trying to make a point. Still, he is right. Most managers don't really know what their teams can achieve. Every year they set these wonderful, aspirational goals that sales people usually know from the beginning are nothing but pie in the sky. The manager doesn't know whether the goal is achievable and there is no roadmap to get to the goal...only the goal itself."

"Yeah. I've seen that over the years." Troy said, "I guess I've done that enough, too. One sales guy says he can increase sales by 10% and I step up and say I can do 15%."

"I call that an ego auction." Alex said, "whoever has the biggest ego wins...until they start having to bring in the results."

"True." Troy said.

"You can't do that when you're a manager, Troy." Alex said quietly, "You have to base your goals on the reality of the situation. That's all Jim was trying to say."

"Fair enough." Troy said. "Where do we start?"

"Start with what success looks like." Alex answered. "How are the regions measured?"

"On sales results." Troy quickly answered.

"Okay." Alex probed further, "How are sales results measured?"

"What do you mean?" Troy asked confused. "Customers order and sales are calculated."

"The only thing that gets measured is sales volume?" Alex asked.

"I'm not following you." Troy answered.

"Well, if sales volume is all that gets measured then the top region is the one with the most sales volume." Alex explained. "Is that how it works here?"

"Well, not exactly." Troy answered, "I think the regions are ranked by sales volume, percentage sales increase and dollar increase."

"Yes." Alex confirmed "You're right. How is the southeast doing on those three parameters?"

"I'm not sure but I think we're in last place across the board." Troy answered.

Alex pulled up the regional rankings on his computer and projected the image onto the screen.

Region	Sales Volume (millions)	Dollar Increase (millions)	Percentage Increase	Overall Rank (ranking score)
Southwest	47.4 (1)	5.5(1)	11.7%(3)	1(5pts)
Central	33.4 (4)	4.6 (2)	13.8%	2(8pts)
Mid-Atlantic	32.6 (5)	4.6 (3)	14.0%	3(9pts)
Western	39.7 (3)	4.3 (4)	10.8%	4(12pts)
Northeast	44.5(2)	3.9(5)	8.7%(6)	5(13pts)
Southeast	29.9(6)	3.5(6)	11.6%(4)	6(16pts)

"Interesting." Troy said, "We are in last place on sales volume, last place on dollar increase and fourth in percentage increase."

"Now look at the top region." Alex said. "How are they doing?"

"The top region is the southwest." Troy observed, "They are first in sales volume, first in dollar increase and third in percentage increase."

"Now let's look at the gap between the southeast and the southwest." Alex said "The difference between the two regions on sales volume is $17.5 million. The difference on dollar growth is $ 2 million. The difference on percentage growth is .1%"

"Wow." Troy said with disappointment, "We can't get there from here. The gap is too large."

"That might be true." Alex said. "But what would it take to get into second place?"

"I'm not sure." Troy answered.

"Well, is it easier for the southeast to win on sales volume, dollar growth or percentage growth?" Alex asked

"Clearly, percentage growth." Troy said looking once again at the rankings. "I don't think we can beat Mid-Atlantic on sales volume, but if we accelerated our percentage growth a bit, we could at least be number one on that parameter."

"I agree." Alex said enthusiastically. "What would that number have to be for the southeast to win on percentage growth?"

"Well, Mid-Atlantic is currently the top district on percentage growth at 14%." Troy answered. "I guess we need to be around 15%"

"Well, let's do the math." Alex said, "If you were growing at 15% your dollar growth would be $ 4.5 million. That would put your ranking in dollar growth in fourth place. But look how close the regions would be right around you. Another $200,000 gain would put you in second place on the parameter of dollar growth."

"Interesting." Troy said as he recalculated. "All it would take is for us to grow our percentage growth to 15.6% and then we would be in second place on dollar growth."

"Yes." Alex said with excitement. "Then the rankings would be very, very different. Let's look."

Region	Sales Volume millions	Dollar Increase millions	Percentage Increase	Overall Rank (ranking score)
Southwest	47.5 (1)	5.5(1)	11.7%(4)	1(6pts)
Southeast	31.1 (6)	4.7 (2)	15.6% (1)	2 (9pts)
Central	33.4 (4)	4.6 (3)	13.8% (3)	3 (10pts)
Mid-Atlantic	32.6 (5)	4.6 (4)	14.% (2)	4 (11pts)
Western	44.5 (2)	4.3 (5)	10.8% (5)	5 (12pts)
Northeast	44.5(3)	3.9(6)	8.7%(6)	6(15pts)

"We would move into second place." Troy said with surprise.

"How much buy-in do you think you would get with your new team by telling them that if they only grew their business by 4 percentage points they would be in second place instead of last place?" Alex asked.

"That's amazing." Troy said, "It seems achievable when you look at it this way."

"Now obviously, this is only the first step." Alex said, "You will need to go further to determine exactly where you can get that gain. As well, you can't expect that the other regions are going to sit back and do nothing."

"True." Troy answered, "But this is logical, and people can relate to logic. It is a very good start."

"What do you think we need to do next?" Alex asked.

"We need to see where we can get that kind of growth." Troy answered.

"Yes." Alex answered. "And to do that we have to look at how your territories are currently stacking up. I think you're going to see some surprises."

Alex pulled up a spreadsheet of the southeast region territories on the screen.

Territory	Sales Volume	% growth	$ growth
Birmingham	$ 1.25	9%	$ 11,250
Mobile	$ 1.21	12%	$ 145,200
North GA	$ 1.20	14%	$ 168,000
Atlanta East	$ 4.15	7%	$ 290,500
Atlanta West	$ 4.22	21%	$ 886,200
Tallahassee	$ 1.75	10%	$ 175,000
Gainesville	$ 1.53	7%	$ 107,100
Jacksonville	$ 1.10	10%	$ 110,000
Tampa Bay	$ 1.39	8%	$ 111,200
Orlando	$ 3.71	19%	$ 704,900
Miami	$ 5.07	11%	$ 557,700
Charlotte, NC	$ 3.31	6%	$ 198,600
SE Region	$ 29.89	11.4%	$ 3,465,000

Alex said, "Tell me what you see."

Troy took his time looking at the spreadsheet. He pulled out his iPad and calculator taking some notes.

"Well, first there are four territories that make more than half of the total sales volume for the southeast region; Miami, Atlanta West, Orlando, and Atlanta East." Troy observed.

"Great observation, Troy." Alex said enthusiastically, "How far down the list do you need to go to capture 80% of your total sales volume?" Alex quickly sorted the spreadsheet by sales volume making the task easier.

"Let's see." Troy said, "seven territories make up 80% of the sales volume."

"Exactly." Alex said, "And look at this. When I add up the total volume of the bottom five territories they are less than the volume of your top two territories; Miami and Atlanta West."

"That's amazing." Troy said.

"Where are you going to go to pick up another $1.2 Million in dollar growth?'

"Well, clearly it should be easier to get it from the large volume territories and particularly those large territories with low percentage growth should be the low-lying fruit." Troy proposed.

"I like the way you think." Alex said, "Atlanta East, Charlotte and Miami should all be delivering greater growth. Moving each of these to your goal of 15.6% growth would get you an additional $900,000. I'm pretty sure that you can find another $300,000 in the remaining nine territories. What do you think?

"Definitely." Troy said enthusiastically. "Let me work on some potential goals for the team that will guarantee that we make our number."

With that Alex excused himself while Troy put together his forecasting plan. A few minutes later he returned, and Troy shared his ideas.

"What did you come up with?" Alex asked.

"First, the minimum standard for the three territories we discussed will have to be 15.6% growth. Then, what I'm going to ask that everyone deliver will follow this schedule." Troy said as he pointed to the white board.

Current Percentage Growth	Added Percentage Needed
20% or above	Add 2%
15-19%	Add 3%
10-14%	Add 4%
Less than 10%	Add 5%

"Of course, anyone can debate the rules," Troy said, "But in the end, we still need to generate additional dollar growth of $ 1.2 Million. This plan would allow us to far exceed that. I'd be open to other business rules that can get us to the same place."

"I like where you're going" Alex said. "Still, you will need to look even more micro to see if there are accounts within each territory that can grow to get to those numbers."

"Well, actually I think each of the sales representatives will need to do that." Troy reflected, "They might need a little help."

"Good point." Alex said. "In fact, you would never set the goals for your sales representatives. You want them to do it themselves. You will want to look at the customer list, though. You have some individual customers that are larger than some of your smallest volume territories."

"Thanks for pointing that out." Troy said with a laugh, "And I bet some of them are in Atlanta."

"And you are right." Alex said with a smile. "There's something else I want you to think about."

"What's that?" Troy asked.

"How much does a single unit of our product cost?" Alex asked.

"Depending on the individual contract, it costs somewhere between $4800 and $5400." Troy answered.

"Look at the difference between the dollar growths each territory currently is showing versus the dollar growth you have put as the goal. How many units does the difference represent?" Alex asked.

"Well obviously it varies." Troy answered, "But I'm looking for a $1.2 million gain divided by $ 5000; that's 240 units. Divide that by 12 territories and we're talking 20 more units per territory."

"Yes." Alex agreed "Spread that out over a year and you're asking for little more than one new unit per month. As Sam Logan likes to say, 'if you can't sell one more unit a month you ought to be arrested for impersonating a sales person.'"

Troy and Alex laughed heartily.

"Can you believe the day is almost over?" Troy asked. "It's already 5:30pm. Where did the day go?"

"I don't know." Alex answered, "But if I were you I'd get a good night's sleep. Jim will be ready to start business planning at 7:30am. It will be an aggressive day, for sure."

As if on cue, Jim came into the conference room.

"How did you do today?" Jim asked.

"We made some real progress." Troy answered.

Jim then asked the same question he asked as soon as Troy arrived earlier in the day. "Can the southeast region be the top region next year?"

"Unless something miraculous happens, the top position is probably not going to happen but the number two spot is totally attainable." Troy said confidently.

Jim seemed to suppress a smile. "You did make progress today." he said. "Tomorrow we will figure out exactly how to make that happen. See you at 7:30am".

QUESTIONS TO CONSIDER:

1) How is your team's performance measured? If market share, profitability or market penetration were key measures would your analytic approach change?

2) What do you need to achieve in the coming year to be the top performing team?

   - How do you compare to the current top team?
   - What is the quickest and easiest way to move up the rankings?

3) Do you expect the same level of performance from each contributor? Why/why not?

4) Can you recall examples of "the ego auction" method of setting objectives from your own experience? What was the outcome?

5) Who in your company can provide fresh insights regarding business analysis?

CHAPTER FIVE: PLANNING FOR "STAR"DOM

When Troy arrived at the office he found Jim and Alex in the conference room going over the numbers generated the day before.

"You did a nice job with setting objectives yesterday, Troy." Jim said barely looking up from the computer. "I'm not sure those are the business rules I would use but they're a far bit better than some I've seen."

Troy put his computer bag on an empty chair and sat down in the adjacent chair.

"You set your growth rate at 15.6%." Jim observed, "What is the market growth the southeast?"

Alex smiled and said quietly, "I bet Troy will be able to think more clearly with a cup of coffee."

"Oh. Of course." Jim said, suddenly aware of his lack of sensitivity, "Sorry, please do go get a cup of coffee. I'm sometimes intense. I'm anxious to get going on your plan "

"No worries." Troy said with a smile. "I'll be right back."

Alex walked with Troy down to the coffee maker. "Jim's alright." Alex said, "You'll get used to him."

Troy smiled thinking about his discussion with Dennis. "Are you familiar with Life's Pie?" Troy asked.

"No, what is it?" Alex asked.

"Oh, never mind. Something Dennis Baker taught me" Troy answered. Troy was thinking about the distribution of

Jim's pie and how it might be one big pie full of work. He chuckled at the thought.

Alex and Troy had entered the conference room when Jim asked the same question as before. "What is the market growth in the Southeast?" Jim queried.

"I'm not sure." Troy answered feeling somewhat incompetent.

"Well, that's something you need to know." Jim said brashly, "What if the market growth is 16% and you're only asking your team to grow 15.6%? Then you'd be asking them to let the competition eat your lunch."

"Wow." Troy answered, "Good point. I hadn't thought of that."

"Well, fortunately I did." Jim answered, "Your market growth is 11.6%. Does that number sound familiar?"

"Sure." Troy answered, "11.6% is our current growth rate."

"Yes." Jim said, "Some might say your team isn't doing a thing except riding the wave of the market."

"I suppose someone might say that." Troy said with a smile

"And essentially, they'd be right." Jim said, "When your growth rate is the same as the market it means that you are neither taking business from the competition nor losing it, instead, you're along for the ride. Now some of your sales representatives are well below the 11.6% market growth. These guys are losing ground to the competition."

"I see what you're saying." Troy acknowledged.

"What are you going to do about it?" Jim challenged.

"I'm going to figure out what's wrong and plan to fix it." Troy said.

"Now that is a darn fine answer." Jim said with a suppressed smile, "but you better figure it out soon. That's part of what we will do today. Part of your business plan might well be to turn around these low growth territories

"That makes sense." Troy acknowledged.

"What do you know about business planning?" Jim asked as an open invitation to ignorance.

"I know the basic structure that we use here. I've done some territory plans over the years but honestly it has always seemed like an exercise you do as a project rather than a roadmap that you actually follow." Troy said tentatively.

"Well, that changes today." Jim said emphatically. "When we're finished you will have a plan that will lead you to the goals you and Alex put together yesterday. Everything in the plan will be followed and I promise you, if you aren't achieving your goals either you have built the wrong plan or are lacking in execution. Both are your responsibility."

Troy's face turned red at the authoritative tone that Jim used yet Jim's self-confidence continued to keep Troy engaged in the conversation. Troy knew that he desperately wanted to succeed, and he needed a good plan to make it happen.

"You said you know the basic structure of a business plan." Jim said, "Why don't you write the components on the flipchart?"

Troy felt intimidated by Jim's style but moved to the flipchart and wrote the following:

Situation Analysis
SWOT
Goal
Strategic Imperative
Tactics
Metrics/Timeline

"Excellent." Jim said, "That is exactly the format we use here. Let's get started."

Jim went to the white board and divided it in half with a marker. One side of the dividing line he labeled, "internal" and the other "external". "Now Troy." Jim said, "I want you to think of everything you know about the southeast region and list each on the internal or external side of the ledger. Remember, internal means anything you control and external are things outside your control. Alex knows a little about the southeast and can help you. I'll be back in a little while to see how you're doing."

Jim left the conference room and Troy looked at Alex and shook his head.

"I feel like I'm back in school." Troy said dejectedly.

"I know that's how Jim comes across." Alex answered, "But stick with this. You're going to love the final product."

Troy took a deep breath. "Okay." He said, "What do we know about the southeast?"

"Why don't we start with what we learned yesterday?" Alex said.

"Okay." Troy started, "We know that four territories account for over half of our sales volume. This means that it should be easy to move dollars if we concentrate our resources. Now that we know market growth we also know we are losing market share in 8 territories. We know that the bottom five territories combined generate less volume than the top two territories combined."

Once Troy and Alex got started they had no problem filling up the entire white board with observations about the southeast team and the business climate. In fact, they were both surprised to find that an hour had passed by the time that Jim came back to the conference room.

Jim looked carefully at the whiteboard which outlined the following:

INTERNAL	EXTERNAL
-8/12 territories losing share	-patient demographic growing 20% in Atlanta, 18% Miami, 12% overall
-4 territories have 60% of total sales volume	-new specialty hospitals opening in North Georgia
-3 sales reps are relatively new hires	-Top hospital in Atlanta becoming "center of excellence" in our disease state
-region under audit	
-lack of trust in leadership	
-several very large customers	
-no regional opinion leaders	- competition has similar sized sales force
-no agreed critical success factors	-competition had 6 sales reps honored at President's Cup equivalent
-no activity metrics	
-resistance to rules/structure	- Medicare considering limitation to coverage in Florida and Georgia
-several low performing tenured reps	
-no top candidates for promotion	- Blue Cross/Blue Shield and Aetna gave preferential status to our product in North and South Carolina.
-1 bitter sales rep. that she wasn't promoted	
-only 1 rep qualified for Presidents Cup	
-culture of complacency?	
-selling skills suspect/service only mentality	
-poor utilization of speaker's programs	
-poor utilization of "new patient kits"	
-no customer targeting program	

"This is a great start guys." Jim said, "Now you divide the factors positive, and neutral issues. Put the positives and negative on the board and delete the neutral issues. This then becomes your initial SWOT analysis"

"Okay." Troy answered. Alex assisted Troy in modifying the white board.

INTERNAL (Positive) STRENGTHS	INTERNAL (Negative) WEAKNESSES
-4 territories have 60% of total sales volume -several very large customers -solid relationships with key customers -mostly tenured team	-8/12 territories losing share -lack of trust in leadership -region under audit- -no regional opinion leaders -no agreed critical success factors -no activity metrics -resistance to rules/structure -several low performing tenured reps - no top candidates for promotion -1 bitter sales rep. that she wasn't promoted - selling skills suspect/service only mentality -poor utilization of speakers' programs -poor utilization of "new patient kits -no customer targeting program (suspect of - calling on friends instead of potential)
EXTERNAL (Positive) OPPORTUNITIES -patient demographic	EXTERNAL (Negative) THREATS - competition had 6 sales reps

growing 20% in Atlanta, 18% Miami, 12% overall -new specialty hospitals opening in North Georgia and -Top hospital in Atlanta becoming "center of excellence" in our disease state - competition has similar sized sales force - BC/BS and Aetna gave preferential status to our product in North and South Carolina.	honored at President's Cup equivalent -Medicare considering limitation to coverage in Florida and Georgia

Jim took a good look at the reorganized table. "Great job, guys." Jim said, "You've created your initial SWOT analysis. I'm surprised at how many weaknesses you have but that indicates a lot of opportunity for improvement"

Jim added, "Now, go back to the SWOT and highlight the issues that you believe are the most important to address to achieve the objective that you set yesterday. Pick no more than two or three in each quadrant. The result will be your final SWOT."

Troy and Alex debated each issue and then settled on the following as most important to achieve the objective:

FINAL SWOT ANALYSIS

STRENGTHS (Positive Internal)	WEAKNESSES (Negative Internal)
-4 territories make up 60% of sales -several very large customers -solid relationships with key customers	-lack of trust in leadership -no activity metrics -selling skills/service only mentality -no customer targeting program
OPPORTUNITIES (Positive External)	THREATS (Negative External)
-patient demographic growing 20% in Atlanta, 18% in Miami, 12% overall -BC/BS and Aetna gave preferential status in Carolinas	-Medicare considering coverage limitation in Florida and Georgia

Jim agreed with the issues highlighted, "I think you have the concept down well enough."

"What do we do next?" Alex asked.

"Well, next we will determine the Strategic Imperatives." Jim answered, "But before we progress I have a question. What's the difference between a strategy and a tactic?"

"Let me take a stab at it." Alex replied, "A strategy is what you're trying to do, and a tactic is how you're doing it?

"Not bad." Jim answered, "How about you, Troy?'

"A strategy is big picture while a tactic is about the details." Troy outlined.

"The truth is you are both right and yet others have different definitions." Jim answered, "In fact I found 19 power point presentations on-line none of which were in perfect agreement. There is a Harvard Business Review article about the simplicity of strategy and tactics. It was 45 pages long. So much for simplicity."

"How do we define it here at Mareno?" Troy asked.

"We don't." Jim answered, "But I think there are some things we can agree on. Each company, brand and region has an annual goal. You worked on yours yesterday. In addition, there are certain big things that must be done to accomplish those goals. For those big things to be achieved there are a series of individual tasks that must be done. Finally, those tasks can usually be measured."

"Yes. That makes sense." Troy answered.

"Well, Strategic Imperatives are the big things that need to be done to accomplish the annual goal" Jim said.

"And then Tactics are the tasks we need to do to accomplish the Strategic Imperatives." Alex observed.

"And we need metrics for the tactics to make sure we're on track." Troy added.

"Exactly, guys." Jim affirmed, "Take a few moments to think through what are the three or four big things that need to be done in the southeast to achieve your annual goal. And I really mean no more than four. Okay?"

"Got it." Troy answered with a smile.

"Okay, I'll be back at lunch." Jim said as he left the conference room.

"Where do we start?" Troy asked.

"Let's go back to the SWOT." Alex answered.

"There are several of these issues that are similar." Alex observed, "The fact that there are several large customers, the fact that patient demographics favor Atlanta and Miami and the fact that there is no methodology for segmenting and targeting customers kind of looks like a big thing to me."

"That's a good catch." Troy agreed, "Maybe our first Strategic Imperative should be something about customer targeting. And some of the parameters we might use would be patient demographic growth, dollar volume of customer and whether we are gaining or losing share."

"What else?" Alex asked.

"There are several issues that relate to third-party coverage." Troy said, "We need a Strategic Imperative around managing this, both on the positive and negative sides of coverage."

"I can see that." Alex agreed. "Another seems to be around sales effectiveness.

"I was thinking the same thing." Troy said enthusiastically, "Improving selling skills, activity metrics and changing the culture might be part of that."

"Wow." Alex said, "I think we've covered everything in the SWOT."

"We make a pretty good team." Troy said with a smile.

Troy went to the flipchart and turned to a blank page. He wrote the following:

STRATEGIC IMPERATIVES:
1) Design and Implement Customer Targeting Initiative
2) Maximize Third Party Coverage Advantages
3) Dramatically Improve Sales Force Effectiveness

When Troy had finished writing Jan entered the conference room bringing in sandwiches and soft drinks.

"Is it noon already?" Troy asked.

"Yes." Jan answered, "I can tell you've really been working hard."

"Yes." Troy answered, "But we still have much to do before I leave today."

Jim entered the conference room. "That's precisely why we will be having a working lunch today."

Jan smiled, "Is there any other kind?" she said as she slipped out the door.

"Okay, then." Jim began, "I see you've made progress with your Strategic Imperatives. Now there are some things you need to know."

"Okay." Troy said cautiously.

"Strategic Imperatives are the requirements or pre-requisites for successful achievement of your goal. They can be either objective or subjective, but they always must meet two tests. These are the test of sufficiency and the test of the non-essential." Jim outlined.

"I'm not sure I know what you're talking about." Troy said

"Well, let's look at your three Strategic Imperatives. Do you consider these three to be the pre-requisites for successful achievement of the goal you set yesterday?"

"Yes." Troy answered.

"And are these Strategic Imperatives objective or subjective?" Jim asked.

"Subjective" Troy answered.

"But the Tactics will probably end up being objective." Alex added.

"Yes. Yes." Jim answered, "You are both right. But do these Strategic Imperatives meet the test of sufficiency?"

"What is the test of sufficiency?" Troy asked.

"The test of sufficiency simply asks one question?" Jim stated, "If we are successful in implementing all of our Strategic Imperatives will that be sufficient to meet our objective?"

"Assuming we achieve each of the Strategic Imperatives then we should make the goal?" Troy restated.

"Exactly" Jim answered.

"I think so." Troy said.

"You're making me cringe again.' Jim replied, "Do you think or do you know?"

"I know that if we do all of this we *should* be successful, but I'm concerned that if I can't create a different culture we *could* still fail."

"Then, what do you need to do?" Jim asked.

"I need to add a Strategic Imperative about creating a culture of trust, respect, confidence and competence" Troy answered.

Troy went to the flipchart and added this new Strategic Imperative.

STRATEGIC IMPERATIVES:
1) Design and Implement Customer Targeting Initiative
2) Maximize Third Party Coverage Advantages
3) Dramatically Improve Sales Force Effectiveness
4) Create a Culture of Trust, Respect, Confidence and Competence

Alex chimed in, "I love that you added that."

"Yes." Jim joined in, "And now I think you meet the test of sufficiency. Now, there is one more test"

"Okay." Troy answered, "What is it?"

"The test of the non-essential." Jim answered.

"What is the test of the non-essential?" Troy asked.

"The test of the non-essential looks at your Strategic Imperatives from the opposite angle." Jim answered. "It asks if it is possible to achieve your goal *without* one of the Strategic Imperatives."

"That's interesting." Troy said, "The only one of these I might challenge is whether it is possible to achieve our goal without Maximizing Third Party Coverage. It might be possible, but I doubt it."

"Then you leave it in." Jim said, "But the test of the non-essential allows you to have a good gut check to make sure you aren't prioritizing something that isn't all that important."

"Thanks for sharing this." Troy stated, "These rules are very helpful."

"Now we're running out of time, but I want you to finish the plan for at least one of your four Strategic Imperatives. Why don't you and Alex come up with the Tactics and Metrics for the first Imperative while I make a few phone calls?"

Alex and Troy had no problem outlining the Key Tactics to achieve the first Strategic Imperative. The steps they agreed would be critical were:

TACTICS FOR STRATEGIC IMPERATIVE #1	
1) Design customer targeting model based on: (within 30 days)	
	a. Customer sales volume
	b. Favorable patient demographics
	c. Growth vs, market
	d. Favorable third-party coverage
2) Provide target lists to Sales Representatives (within 60 days)	
3) Set Call Plan objectives by consensus (within 65 days)	
4) Measure Call plan objective attainment (2nd Qtr.)	
5) Analyze Call Plan Metrics against sale results (qtrs. 2,3,4)	
METRICS AND TIMELINES:	
Key Metric:	
	o Region achievement of at least 80% Call Plan attainment
Timeline:	
	o As noted above

When Jim returned to the conference room he looked at the work Troy and Alex had accomplished. "Good work, guys." He complimented.

"I feel like I've learned much today." Troy said, "For the first time I've created a plan that actually leads somewhere. Of course, I've got to work on the other three Strategic Imperatives and complete the Tactics and Metrics to go along with them."

"Yes." Jim said, "This is a great starting point to help instill confidence from the very beginning with your team. There's one other thing I want to share with you before you go."

"Sure." Troy said, "What's on your mind?"

"You outlined one primary metric for the first Strategic Imperative, right?" Jim asked.

"Yes." Troy answered, "Call Plan Attainment."

"If you end up with one or two metrics for each of the four Strategic Imperatives how will you keep track of all of those measures?"

"I know the answer to that one." Alex answered. enthusiastically, "You put them on a region dashboard. I can help Troy do that. I have a special computer program designed for dashboards."

Troy understood that a "dashboard" is a term that describes the various measures and metrics needed to make sure that the business is staying on track. Like the dashboard of an automobile the business dashboard has gauges and warning lights to help the manager know that everything is running smoothly toward the objectives.

"Alex is exactly right." Jim added, "Once you determine all of the metrics and you believe they adequately inform how well you're achieving all of your Strategic Imperatives, the Dashboard is a constant reminder to the entire region as to the importance of your Business Plan to the successful achievement of your objective."

"I can see how that would work." Troy said.

Jan opened the conference room door and poked her head inside. "Troy, your car is here to take you to the airport."

"Okay." Troy said with a smile, "Thank you, Jan."

Troy then turned to both Jim and Alex.

"I can't thank you guys enough." Troy said with genuine warmth, "I owe you both so much."

"Oh, save your sensitive side for the national sales meeting next week." Jim said suppressing a smile, "Believe me, when you meet your southeast team you're going to need all the emotional intelligence you can muster."

"It was a pleasure, Troy." Alex added.

Jim reached across the conference table, shook Troy's hand and made one last comment.

'Good luck, Troy." Jim said, "You're going to make a fine regional manager."

QUESTIONS TO CONSIDER:

1) What growth rates do you benchmark?

2) Is your team gaining, losing or holding market share?

3) What are the internal issues impacting your business?

4) What external issues are impacting your business?

5) Which are positive? Which are negative?

6) How will you determine your Strategic Imperatives?

7) How will you use the "Test of Sufficiency"?

8) How will you use the "Test of the Non-essential"?

9) What metrics belong on your Dashboard?

CHAPTER SIX: MEETING WITH THE "STARS"

Following his trip to the west coast, Troy could think of nothing but the first meeting with his new team. This would be his first opportunity to establish a new culture in the southeast region. He knew that the old expression is true; "you don't get a second chance to make a first impression."

Prior to the national sales meeting, Troy called Greta Martina, the director of human resources.

"Greta, this is Troy Noble." Troy said when Greta answered the phone.

"Troy." Greta said enthusiastically, "Glad to hear from you. How's the new job going?"

"Honestly, it's a whirlwind right now." Troy answered, "As you know, next Monday night everyone will be travelling for the start of the national sales meeting on Tuesday and it will be the first time I will meet members of my new team. I was hoping I could get some advice from you."

"Sure." Greta said, "What can I help you with?"

"Several things." Troy answered, "I'd like to know anything you might think is helpful about the team, some of the team members, what to expect and probably most of all what you think they will be looking for from me."

Greta laughed, "That's a big list. Why don't we start with the last question? What do you think they will be looking for?"

"I've been thinking a lot about that." Troy answered. "I think they will probably be looking for my vision. Maybe, a plan that will take them into the future. They will be wondering if have the knowledge I need to be a leader: especially since I've been at Mareno a relatively short time. They will probably want to know my expectations."

Greta chuckled. "That is quite a bit to cover." She said. "And you may have time for all of that on Tuesday but there is something much more basic they are looking for."

"What's that?" Troy asked, wondering what he had missed.

"They will be looking at who you are as a person." Greta answered, "They will simply want to know if you're a good guy."

"How can I tell them that?" Troy asked.

"You can't." Greta said, "But you can show them. Let me ask you something. What's important to you?"

"Lots of things." Troy answered, "Heather is important to me. Trying to do a good job is important. My spirituality is important."

"And what do you do for fun?" Greta continued.

"I play tennis." Troy said, "And Heather and I like to take bicycle trips. And we love to travel, especially to the mountains. Biking is really fun for us."

"Are you smiling right now?" Greta asked.

"Yes, why do you ask that?" Troy inquired.

"Because I can hear it in your voice." Greta answered, "The tenseness is gone and instead you are more relaxed. That always happens when we talk about our families and our life outside of work."

"Your point is that I need to talk about these things on Tuesday in my breakout session at the national sales meeting?" Troy asked.

"My point is that if you relax and show your team who you really are they are naturally going to be more open." Greta said, "How you do that is up to you, but they need to see that you are a real person; not just their new boss. That will start the minute they begin meeting you at the cocktail reception Monday night."

"That makes sense." Troy said.

"You have to remember that you're worried about how they will respond to you, but each of them is worried about what you will think of them. You must somehow get out of your own head and instead be empathic about their feelings. You've been in their shoes. When you've met a new supervisor, what were you thinking?"

Troy thought about this. "I've thought different things at different times. When I was performing poorly I was afraid the new manager would see me as a liability. Other times, I was a little bit jealous that the new manager was picked for the role instead of me. Still other times, I've been thinking about what I could learn from the new manager."

"And there are twelve of them." Greta said, "Each of them is thinking something different. Put them at ease and you will be at ease."

Troy thought about Dennis sharing the article on "The Tough Day" and how he had Troy read it the second time to think about the seven people being laid off instead of thinking of the manager. Greta was asking him to do the same thing.

"That's good perspective, Greta." Troy said, "Thanks for that."

"Your number one priority in your first team meeting on Tuesday is to begin to establish trust and respect. Your vision, your expectations, your plan, your credibility all will follow if you first begin to build trust."

Before ending their conversation, Troy discussed the new competency model Greta had been designing. Troy was sure that he might be able to incorporate some of this into his meeting agenda.

"Greta, you've been helpful." Troy said, "Thank you."

"Anytime, Troy." she answered, "I'll be at the national sales meeting. I can't wait to hear how things went."

Troy sat at his desk and wrote the following goals for the first team meeting:

1) Establish relationships
2) Set the foundation for trust and respect
3) Create new vision/ establish new goals
4) Discuss mutual expectations

Troy decided that if those four goals were to be accomplished at the national sales meeting, his new team would be off to a very good start.

The national sales meeting started on Monday evening with everyone arriving at the Renaissance Boston Waterfront hotel for a reception. Thanks to Greta sending Troy a pictorial roster, he could recognize many from his new team and strike up conversations. In fact, except for two of the sales representatives who were arriving late Troy could have brief conversations with the entire team.

When the reception was over Troy went back to his room and wrote some of his observations into a password protected file on his iPad:

The STAR Manager

- Cindy Sherman: tenured, proud, works Atlanta East
- Sammy Sherill: works Atlanta West, bragged about "carrying the entire Atlanta market"
- Cassy Clair: tenured, shy, talked about new baby
- Danny Bowman lectured about changing environment at Mareno
- Yolanda Jenner: new, enthusiastic
- Gil Patel- quiet, respectful
- Lester Rivera- little eye contact, seemed down or depressed
- Terri Rodriguez- impressive, bright, positive
- Rodney Rale- likes to ride his Harley, spoke favorably about team

Troy made a ledger with the locations and tenure of each of the team members in the southeast region:

Tenure	Name	Location
New	Yolanda Jenner	Birmingham
5 years	Gil Patel	Tallahassee
8 years	Danny Bowman	Gainesville
2 years	Lester Rivera	Tampa Bay
2 years	Pam Smith	Jacksonville
3 years	Cynthia Sims	North GA
4 years	Rodney Rale	Mobile
4 years	Marty Manzel	Charlotte, NC
7 years	Cindy Sherman	Atlanta East
5 years	Cassy Clair	Orlando
8 years	Sammy Sherrill	Atlanta West
4 years	Terri Rodriguez	Miami

The following morning Troy was up early and already in the breakout room prior to general session to make sure everything would be perfect when the teams dispersed to the regional breakouts. He was so excited that he didn't even eat breakfast. Troy prepared some of his flipchart aids for his breakout room and then hurried to greet his team members as they came down to the "main tent".

Mareno spared no expense for the opening presentation. The stage covered the entire span of the front of the meeting room with a background built to look like the skyline of Boston with the theme written in huge block letters, "A New Era of Excellence".

Stirring inspirational music blared through enormous speakers while the attendees filed into the meeting room and continued to greet each other while finding seats.

Suddenly the music temporarily stopped, and a booming voice announced, "Ladies and gentlemen, please welcome to the stage your Vice President of Sales, Sam Logan."

The roar of applause and cheers was enthusiastic as Sam briskly walked to the stage. Using no podium but rather walking to the edge of the stage, Sam faced front and center to the excited audience.

"It is a beautiful thing to look out at one of the top sales forces in all of healthcare." Sam called out over the microphone to thunderous applause. He waited for the noise to abate, "And even a greater thing to see the sales organization who will take Mareno Biosciences to a billion-dollar company over the next two years." The sales audience again applauded but also had a collective look of shock at such a lofty goal."

"Yes, I know what some of you are thinking." Sam continued, "You're thinking that either I'm crazy or that we've all been smoking something funny up here in Boston."

The audience nervously laughed.

"Well, I *am* crazy." Sam said, "I'm crazy enough to believe that with our current growth trajectory and with the introduction of a new product early next year; yes, you heard me correctly. We will become a billion-dollar organization..."

The audience screamed their excitement of having a new product.

"We have signed a deal for a companion product to our Marenodiatrome that will move us into a market three times our current size; a product so unique that If you can't sell a billion ..."

The sales representatives all joined in to one of Sam's favorite phrases, "then we should be arrested for impersonating a sales force."

"Yes, you should." Sam bellowed a hearty laugh.

Troy couldn't remember much of what else was said in the opening session. All he could think about was how to get the southeast region up and running for the biggest opportunity they might ever see. A new product meant that going from sixth to first might be possible after all. He began thinking whether to adjust his story to the region now that this new piece of information had been revealed.

All too soon, the voice came over the loud speakers, "Ladies and gentlemen, we will now take a short break and you are to report to your breakout rooms by 10:30am."

Troy's heart was thumping in his chest as he made his way back to the regional breakout room.

As each member of Troy's new team arrived, he greeted them personally and made small talk, smiling and shaking hands. It wasn't long until the whole team had filtered in. It was interesting to Troy how the sales representatives chose their seats. Danny and Sammy were as far from the front of the room as possible. The newbie, Yolanda sat near the front of the room. Then there were those who clustered together because of their geographic alignment. The Georgia sales representatives Cynthia and Cindy sat near the middle of the room while Terri, Cassy and Pam from Florida sat together near the front. The others seemed to sit where ever the remaining seats were available.

Troy started with an icebreaker asking everyone to write down on a chart where they were originally from, the thing they most like to do for fun and finally, if they were in a circus, what animal they would be.

The team seemed to have a great time listening to each member discuss their interests and circus animal aspirations. When it was Troy's turn he said the following. "I'm originally from Cleveland which should explain why I don't brag much about sports." There was some polite laughter.

"One of Heather and my favorite things is taking bicycle trips. We are those annoying people you see in groups of 40-50 that take up the whole road and slow everybody down. And yes, I promise you right now that you will never have to see me stuff my increasingly fat belly into one of those obnoxious cycling outfits."

There were some more polite laughs.

"As for a circus animal, I think I feel like one of those seals that has to balance a huge ball on his nose; only the ball is everything we must do as a team. I'm not sure if I can keep everything balanced...I sure hope I can count on you to help me." Troy said with a big, toothy smile.

Everyone seemed to like the fact that Troy could be honest about his misgivings about the tasks of his job.

When everyone was seated, Troy walked to the front of the room and revealed two pre-drawn flipchart pages. One had a big red #6 scrawled across while the other had #1 in orange.

Troy opened with a question. "Who can tell me what these two numbers represent?"

Danny, one of the tenured representatives who complained the previous night spoke loudly and somewhat sarcastically, "the six represents where we currently stand as a region and the #1 is where you, as our new leader plan to take us. We've read this book before."

Troy kept his cool and laughed. "Danny, as much as I wish it were that easy, I'm afraid that might be a bit lofty for where we are now." Troy said with a smile "but I like the way you think. Anyone else know what the #6 and #1 represent?"

The entire group seemed to breathe more freely as Troy seemed undisturbed by what could have been a tense moment.

No one spoke up as Troy smiled warmly looking around the room.

"Last year Vista Bioscience, our largest competitor rewarded six of their representatives in their southeast region with their Chairman's Award. I've heard that they had an amazing award's trip to Cabo San Lucas. That's what the #6 stands for."

Troy paused to let this fact sink in.

"What do you think the #1 stands for?" Troy then asked

Cynthia called out, "That only one of our team made it to President's Cup?"

"Exactly." Troy answered. "It's one thing as Danny pointed out when we lose out in comparison to the other teams within Mareno, but it is totally unacceptable to lose out to the Vista people. I've met almost all of you one-on-one and this I know. You are far better than the people I've met at Vista. Of course, we would like to rise to the top of the ranks of Mareno together but next year I want these two numbers to be reversed. I want at least six of you to be present at President's Cup and I want the sales representatives at Vista to be at home licking their wounds."

Troy looked around the room and was pleased to see several heads nodding in agreement.

"Now, I must tell you, I've been working over the past week with some of the best business minds within Mareno to try to figure out how we go from where we are to where we have the capability of going. I think you're going to be surprised at how possible it is to move up the rankings. I also think that the competition at Vista is going to be shocked at how quickly we start eating their lunch."

Over the course of the next hour, Troy outlined the analysis and plan that he had prepared with Alex and Jim. Most of the team seemed to "buy in" to the plan and even showed excitement about getting started. Still others, particularly Danny Bowman and Sammy Sherrill looked skeptical.

Troy looked directly at Sammy and asked him a question. "Sammy, you've no doubt seen a lot of plans come and go. What are your thoughts?"

"Honestly, I'm skeptical." He answered, "I don't mean to be critical, but you've only been here for two years. I'm not sure you know enough for us to follow your ideas for success."

The entire room fell silent as several of the team members looked very uncomfortable with the confrontation. Troy however, remained upbeat and calm.

"Sammy, I want to thank you for saying what a lot of people are probably thinking." Troy began, "I've been in the audience when a new manager has come in and I've thought the same thing. The truth is that I don't have a perfect answer for your concerns yet. At the beginning, we've got to give each other the benefit of the doubt. We have to try to trust each other."

"Yeah, that didn't work out so well the last time." Danny Bowman said under his breath.

Ignoring the comment, Troy asked. "What do you think will build trust in each other?"

"Time" Danny said out loud.

"Consistency." Cynthia added.

"Actions aligning with words" Gil added.

"Yes." Troy said, "And alignment to the expectations we have of each other."

"Here we go." Danny said, "Another manager's expectations."

"Maybe eventually." Troy answered, "But right now I'm talking about your expectations of me." Can we break into three groups? I would like each group to outline the top expectations that you have for me. Then we will get back together and have each group share."

The groups worked hard as evidenced from the level of noise in the room as each team discussed what they expected from a manager. Troy stayed completely out of these discussions but couldn't wait to hear the outcome.

When Troy reconvened the session following a short break he had each group flipchart their expectations. After each group presented there were seven expectations listed. These were:

- <u>Honesty</u>- *providing honest feedback and communicating the truth; if not able to share, explain why*
- <u>Confidentiality</u>- *anything shared personally or discussions around performance should not be shared with others in the team*
- <u>Advocacy</u>- *when issues need to be shared with company, manager should act as an advocate*
- <u>Dependability</u>- *keep appointments and promises*
- <u>Accessibility</u>- *answer phone whenever possible, return text messages and answer emails within reasonable time*
- <u>Personal integrity</u>-*don't expect special privileges and don't do improper things while on the job*
- <u>Flexibility</u>- *whenever it doesn't negatively impact the company or team, be flexible with personal circumstances*
-

Troy listened, asked questions and asked for examples to ensure that he understood the expectations of the team. He then thanked the team for their work.

"I really want to thank you all for helping me to understand what you are looking for in a manager." Troy said, "I will strive to always uphold these standards but if you ever feel that I have failed, I need your commitment to confront me openly and honestly."

The team all agreed. Then Yolanda spoke up. "What are your expectations of us?"

Troy looked back at the list the team had given him. "I'm sure over time we will develop specific standards that can help us achieve our goals together, but I would have a hard time coming up with a better list of expectations than you have provided to me. Some of the definitions might be a little bit different but the standards are hard to beat. I think the only thing I might add is that I expect you to do the best job that you can; that you always strive for excellence. And you should expect that from me, as well."

The relationship between Troy and the southeast team seemed to be off to a good start. Now the real work would begin.

QUESTIONS TO CONSIDER:

1) What have you done to build trust and respect within your team? If you don't yet manage a team what do you do with your peers to build trust and respect?

2) How would different members of your team or your peers describe your personality?

3) What expectations do your team members have of you? What feedback have you been given?

4) What expectations do you have of your team members? What feedback have you provided to them?

CHAPTER SEVEN: THE NORTH "STAR"

The national meeting ended late afternoon on Thursday and the Boston weather turned nasty; a daunting and flight-delaying mixture of fog and thunderstorms. It was 8:30pm when the airline finally called Troy's flight for boarding. As Troy settled into his seat for the short flight back to Cleveland he reflected on the national sales meeting and particularly his breakout session with his new team. Troy thought of the four goals he had set for this first exposure to his team satisfied that each was accomplished.

While there was still much to do Troy believed that the meeting was a positive first step for the team.

The new goal that Sam put in front of the sales force to achieve $1 billion in sales in two years along with the introduction of a new product was invigorating. It was also overwhelming.

Troy could almost hear Dennis saying, "Which piece of your pie got larger?" Troy smiled remembering the lesson of "Life's Pie" and he thought he should give Heather a great deal of attention when he got back to Cleveland.

When he pulled up to the house at almost 11:00pm Troy was surprised that Heather wasn't waiting up for him but had already gone to bed. He found a note in the kitchen that she had placed with a magnet on the refrigerator door."

"Troy, I love you. There's some fried chicken in the fridge. Sorry, I went to bed early. I have a cold and I'm exhausted from getting things done for the move. Looks like we will get an early closing. We can probably move within a month. See you tomorrow, Sweetie. Love, Heather"

"So much for Life's Pie", Troy thought with a smile. He opened the refrigerator, pulled out a chicken leg and can of beer and sat in a darkened living room. Even though Troy was worn out from the past few days, his mind needed slow down before he would be able to fall asleep.

When Troy woke up at 9am the next morning, he jumped out of bed in a panic thinking he had overslept. He was halfway to the shower when he realized that it was Friday morning and that he would be working from home. Troy quickly showered and dressed before going downstairs for a cup of coffee.

He found Heather in the kitchen fixing him eggs and bacon. Troy came up behind her and put his arms around her, kissing her neck and breathing in the fresh scent of her hair.

"I've missed you, Baby." Troy whispered.

"Missed you too." she whispered with a sigh.

"How's the cold?" Troy asked.

"Much better." Heather said, "Just a sniffle left."

The two of them sat down to eat breakfast when Troy's cell phone started vibrating on the table.

"Oh Baby, can't you let it go to voicemail?" Heather said.

The phone continued to buzz and then finally stopped. Heather looked up at Troy and smiled longing for connection. Then less than a minute later the phone began buzzing again.

Troy looked at his phone and saw the caller ID digital display. It read, "Sam Logan".

"It's Sam." Troy said apologetically, "I better get this."

Heather looked frustrated as Troy took the call.

"Hi Sam." Troy said as he answered the phone. "What's going on?"

"I was about to ask you the same thing." Sam answered.

"Why?" Troy said.

"Have you checked your email yet?" Sam asked.

"Actually, I had a late flight last night and I just got up." Troy said a bit too defensively.

"Yeah, I know." Sam said, "I heard everyone got out late. Anyway, you had two resignations this morning."

"Two?" Troy said shocked, "But I thought the session this week went really well. Who resigned?"

"Marty Mansell and Gil Patel." Sam said, "Honestly, I don't really care that Mansell left. He's never had great results, but Gil seems like a good guy. It looks bad for two people to leave this early."

"Did they say why they are quitting?" Troy asked.

"Same old stuff, left for better opportunity, better pay that kind of thing." Sam said, "Read the emails. I've got to go but you should check things out. Make sure you don't have a mutiny going on. Talk later."

Troy didn't even have time to answer. Sam was already gone.

"What's going on?" Heather asked.

"I'm not sure." Troy answered, "Two of my people already resigned. I better go upstairs and make some phone calls"

Heather remained at the breakfast table wanting to be supportive but already fighting feelings of jealousy about Troy's job.

Troy opened his email and found 115 messages awaiting him. He scrolled down to find the two letters of resignation. Troy read each of them trying to see what messages each conveyed. Seeing nothing unusual, Troy picked up his phone and called Marty first.

When Marty answered he was cordial. "Hi Troy, what's going on?" Marty answered.

"Marty, I got your email." Troy started, "I don't understand. Why are you leaving?"

"Man, it's time." Marty said, "The company is changing, and the job isn't as much fun as it used to be. Seems like everyone is checking up on us all the time. My brother-in-law has been bugging me for years to go in with him on a new venture. We started the company a couple of months ago. Now he needs me to step up and work with him full time. It's nothing personal."

"Can you help me understand something?" Troy asked, "What did you mean that it seems like everyone is checking up on you? Have I done something that makes you feel that way?"

"No, it's not you." Marty said, "That woman from finance sent a notice that my expense reports were being audited and some guy I've never heard of from compliance wanted to set up a call with me. I don't need that kind of stuff. Life is stressful enough without your company being on your tail all the time."

"Marty." Troy asked, "Are you pretty solid in your decision?"

"Definitely." Marty answered, "But I appreciate your call. You seem like a pretty good guy. But don't expect that mine will be the last resignation. There are a few others that are getting the same kind of pressure from home office and I think they might leave too."

"Thanks for the heads up, Marty." Troy said, "And good luck in your new business. Keep in touch."

Troy was about to call Sarah about the expense audit when his phone rang again. This time it was Gil Patel.

"Gil." Troy said when he answered the phone, "I was about to call you."

"I wanted to call and say thanks." Gil said.

"Thanks?" Troy asked confused, "For what?"

"For getting the team to believe again." Gil said, "I don't know how much you know about how things were before, but it was really bad."

"What are you talking about?' Troy asked.

"We were all asked to do things by our old boss that we didn't feel good about." Gil said.

"Like what?" Troy asked.

"Some of us were asked to circumvent some of the company rules by buying gift cards and giving them to the old boss to use with top customers."

"And you did this?" Troy asked.

"Yes." Gil said, "I did it several times. Each time I put four $25 entries into miscellaneous and bought cards to give to my boss."

"Have you told anyone about this?" Troy asked.

"No and I promise I won't." Gil said, "That's why I'm leaving the company. There's an expense audit and I think this is going to come out anyway."

"Gil, you have to come forward and tell what you know." Troy said, "I'm going to call our compliance officer to have him reach out to you. I truly appreciate you telling me about this but now we have to get the issue in the right hands; okay?"

"Troy, I don't know how many people were involved." Gil said, "What if people lose their jobs?"

"Gil." Troy said calmly, "This kind of thing defines who we are. You and I both know what the right thing is to do and we're going to do it."

"Troy." Gil said, "I think I would have really liked working with you."

"Likewise, Gil" Troy answered.

When Troy hung up the phone his head was spinning. Who should he call and what should he do? Sam needed to know about this. Sarah, the VP of finance probably already knew. Greta in human resources was clearly going to be impacted. If customers were being given gift cards this had implications for compliance that could put the company in jeopardy.

Troy sent a text message to Sam. "I need to talk to you ASAP."

The text had barely been sent when Troy's phone rang. Troy outlined to Sam everything that he had been told by Gil and Marty. Sam told Troy to stay put while he had Deirdre set up a conference call between key personnel.

In a matter of a few minutes, the conference call was scheduled between Sam, Sarah, Greta, Tom Whitmore, the vice president of compliance and Frank Delaney, one of the company attorneys.

Tom opened the call.

"First, Troy I want to thank you for coming forward with the information that prompted this call. You absolutely did the right thing by calling Sam." Tom began, "This is not entirely new information to many of us on this call. We have been investigating the southeast region's last three months of expenses. Your predecessor, Brian left the company rather abruptly and in his quick departure left some clues behind about some irregularities which I am not free to discuss.

To make a long story short, there appeared to be some possible compliance violations. To investigate more thoroughly I asked Sarah to do a complete audit on the expense reports from the southeast.

There were many concerning entries; several which appeared to be isolated events while others were well orchestrated and persistent. While we were not quite ready to bring Sam in on what disciplinary actions were needed, we had identified three sales representatives where we believe culpability to be quite strong. Marty and Gil were two of the three. Cynthia Sims is the other. We believe that others might have participated with 'one off entries' but these could not be proven short of an actual confession by the employee."

Sam promptly jumped in, "Why don't we fire anyone we suspect?"

"That would put us at a great deal of risk regarding unlawful discharge suits." Frank answered.

"Then what do we do, bring in each sales representative and try to get a confession?" Sarah asked.

Greta spoke up, "It sounds like you've done a thorough investigation and that the three individuals most culpable have been identified. Two of them have already resigned. The third we will also need to terminate employment. As for the rest of the team, I think the best approach would be to acknowledge the situation, specify that the company won't tolerate any non-compliant behavior moving forward and then educate the group on compliance and personnel rules."

"That sounds like a plan." Sam agreed, "Any dissention to that?"

No one on the call disagreed.

"Let's do this on Monday." Sam continued, "Troy, get in touch with your team and schedule a mandatory meeting at noon. Have Cynthia Sims come in first thing, though. We will need to terminate her employment prior to the group meeting."

"Don't you think we should keep Troy out of this?' Greta asked, "You know, since he's new?"

"Absolutely not." Sam billowed, "Troy's the leader of this team and he needs to be the one carrying this forward. Don't you agree Troy?"

"I completely agree." Troy said, "I talked a lot about honesty and integrity at the meeting earlier this week. This is where I can demonstrate that honesty."

The call ended with a meeting agenda being finalized. Troy would open the meeting, Greta and Tom would provide compliance and human resources education and finally, Sam would close the meeting by Skype outlining his expectations for the future.

Troy spent Friday afternoon contacting the members of the southeast team and preparing for the Monday meeting. He stumbled downstairs from his office just past 6:30pm. Heather looked up from reading on her iPad as Troy came down the stairs.

"Let's go out to dinner." Troy said, "I feel like we haven't been together for a month."

Heather jumped up at the invitation. "Can you leave the phone behind?" She asked. Troy took the phone from his pocket and tossed it in the kitchen drawer.

The weekend seemed like a blur for Troy and Heather. Saturday, they ran errands together while discussing their move to Atlanta. On Sunday, they went to church followed by Sunday brunch. Afterward, it was back to the house, so Troy could pack for his late afternoon flight to Atlanta.

"I promise it won't be like this forever." Troy said as he kissed Heather good-bye. "Once we get settled in Atlanta everything will get much better."

Heather believed such promises less and less. She knew that once they moved she would settle into a new job and a new routine while Troy was becoming increasingly consumed by his new management position.

Troy slept little on Sunday night. Thoughts of the meeting with Cynthia Sims and the larger meeting with the entire team prevented his mind from rest.

Interestingly, the meeting with Cynthia was not as challenging as Troy would have anticipated. Greta and Tom went step by step through the expense violations which were revealed by the audit. When they finished, Greta asked Cynthia if there was anything she wanted to share.

"Look, I knew what we were doing was wrong from the beginning." Cynthia said, "But one of the customers Brian was giving the gift cards to was in my territory. I felt trapped, but I also knew that sooner or later someone was going to find out. I guess my only question now is whether you will let me resign instead of firing me?"

Greta pulled out a piece of blank paper and allowed Cynthia to write her resignation. The meeting closed without incident.

The larger meeting with the team was more challenging. Greta informed Troy that there were some rules they must follow:

1) They could not state the exact nature of the violations
2) They could not infer guilt of any of the departing employees including the former southeast region manager
3) They could not promise that further actions would not be taken

Troy agreed to each of these rules even though he had to amend much of what he had been thinking about saying to the team.

Instead of being in the meeting room to greet each person as they arrived, Troy entered after everyone had been seated. Unlike a week earlier when the room was filled with chatter and small talk this meeting room was as silent as a library.

Troy walked to the front of the room and virtually every set of eyes was upon him.

Troy looked around the room in silence before speaking.

"Obviously, this is not a routine team meeting." Troy acknowledged, "Our primary topic is one that is serious and greatly concerning. Less than a week ago, when we were together in Boston, we spoke about expectations and standards. Some of the expectations you had of me were honesty, confidentiality, dependability and personal integrity. I'm hoping today that we will demonstrate to each other that these are values that we really believe in; values that we will always live up to in our work together."

The room remained silent like a courtroom where a verdict is about to be read. Troy however, went off in a new direction.

"You know that the company has been working over the past several months to determine performance standards for the sales force." Troy said, clearly causing his team to wonder where he was going with this topic. "Many of you have participated in surveys from HR on this."

Troy looked up at Greta who was unprepared to be called upon. "Greta." Troy asked.

"What are the four big buckets of skills needed to be successful in sales at Mareno?"

Greta spoke quietly, "The four areas are Relationship Management, Territory Management, Product/Market Knowledge and Selling Skills."

"Yes." Troy said, "I'm sure none of us would debate that these are necessary for sales success. In fact, looking around this room I see several of you who have done exceptional jobs with these four attributes."

Troy paused, the silence prominent.

"And yet." Troy continued, "Even if someone is absolutely perfect with all four, that person could still fail and cause the whole company to fail, as well. We are a healthcare company. We earn our living by providing products that help people heal. People put their trust in us. They expect us to sell our products ethically, without influencing healthcare decision-makers in inappropriate ways. They expect us to follow the law. They expect us to do the right thing."

Troy once again paused, taking his time to look eye to eye with each team member.

"The problem is." He continued, "The southeast region hasn't always done the right thing, have we? The problem is that our expense management hasn't been honest at times and that our business behavior may not have always been ethical and appropriate, especially for those entrusted with doing the right thing for the patients who need our products. I want to make one thing completely clear. Moving forward, I promise that I will hold each of you to a standard of utmost integrity and I expect that you will hold me to that same standard. We cannot tolerate in each other any compromise involving our ethics and the law.

The southeast region recently underwent a complete expense audit and there were many concerns which arose from that audit. The audit is now finished, and individual issues have been addressed but I've told Sarah, our vice president of finance and Tom, our vice president of compliance that our books will remain open and transparent for anyone who might want to confirm the ethics of the southeast region moving forward. Personal integrity must become our 'north star'; the thing we follow always regardless of circumstance. Now I have one question for everyone in this room. Will you commit to absolute personal integrity moving forward?"

"Yes." the group said together.

Ignoring the group's confirmation, Troy went person by person around the room.

"Do I have your commitment, Yolanda?" Troy asked.

"Yes." Yolanda answered.

"Do I have your commitment, Sammy?" Troy asked.

"Yes." Sammy answered.

"Do I have your commitment Cassy?"

"Yes. Troy. You have my commitment." Cassy answered.

Troy continued until he received a clear "yes" from every single member of the team.

The meeting continued according to agenda with training conducted by both compliance and human resources. At three pm, Troy opened his laptop and called up the Skype application placing Sam's image on the screen at the front of the room. Sam was seated at his desk in Boston.

Sam didn't look happy.

"Any of you who know me," Sam began, "know how disappointed I am to even be having this conversation with you. I'm used to being proud of the members of my sales force; not embarrassed by their behaviors that put themselves and this company at risk. Some of your peers are no longer with us because of these kinds of antics and I promise you that if you think you can get by with cheating and breaking our rules, I will have no problem firing you. Each of you better make a choice and you better make it right now. You can either choose to do the right thing and stay here or you can choose the wrong way. If you choose the wrong way you will not be a part of Mareno Bioscience." Sam reached over to snuff out the Skype application.

Sam's words permeated the room like a dense, zero-visibility fog. The efforts of Greta and Tom to make the day seem more about healing than punishment disappeared in less than thirty seconds.

Troy went to the front of the room looking at the stunned look on each face in the audience.

Troy smiled slightly and said, "Now that's what my granddaddy from Texas used to call getting a whooping."

There was some nervous laughter.

"I want you to listen to me." Troy said in an uncharacteristically quiet voice, "Yesterday is behind us.

We are not even the same southeast region that we were before. What matters is not what we were but what we are going to become. Every day we have a chance to make great choices. Every day we have the chance to be what we can be. I don't believe in what is already gone by. I believe in the team we are going to be now. Let's learn our lessons from this but we cannot afford to let this consume us. Let's make this our new beginning."

The team clapped their hands together rhythmically, louder and louder, and then suddenly everyone stopped.

Troy adjourned the meeting then shook each person's hand as they filed out of the room.

Troy looked at Greta and Tom. "Are there rules against having a drink before five pm?" He asked.

"I'm going to go with the 'it's five o'clock somewhere' excuse." Greta said with a sigh.

"I can't argue that one." Tom said in agreement.
The three of them went to the concierge lounge upstairs.

"You were impressive today, Troy." Tom observed, "I really loved the north star comment about personal integrity."

"Thanks." Troy answered, "But I was flying by the seat of my pants."

Greta chimed in, "If that's the case you handle stress really well."

"No, stress is what happens next." Troy said.

"Why do you say that?" Greta asked.

"Because now I have three vacancies and absolutely no experience hiring anyone." Troy answered.

"I'm staying over tonight in Atlanta." Greta said, "Why don't we meet for breakfast before I go back to Boston and we can talk about what you need to do to get started."

Troy's phone beeped indicating he had a text message.

He glanced at the message from Dennis. The text simply said, "Which piece got bigger?"

"Anything important?" Greta asked.

"A text from Dennis Baker reminding me to call my wife."

QUESTIONS TO CONSIDER:

1) If you had a crisis of this nature whom would you involve?

2) Would you have advocated for Marty or Gil to stay?

3) Would your team say personal integrity is your "north star"?

4) What did you think of Sam's message? How would you help your team recover?

5) Would you challenge Sam about his impact on your team? How would you address the issue?

CHAPTER EIGHT: FINDING THE STARS

Troy met Greta at 7:30am in the concierge suite where a light breakfast buffet was already prepared. There were only a couple of other people in the lounge making it conducive to conversation. After filling their plates and getting a cup of coffee the two sat at a small table in the corner away from the television at the other end of the lounge.

"You now have another responsibility on your shoulders; recruiting new sales representatives." Greta said starting the conversation.

"Yes." Troy said, "And I honestly don't know how to go about it. Any suggestions?"

"Several." Greta answered, "First, I would suggest you get together with Buzz Hill from the mid-atlantic region. Buzz has been in the regional manager's role for about 3 years. He came into a similar mess when he took over. He had to replace seven representatives in the first few months. He should be able to provide some interesting perspective since he made some good choices and others that didn't turn out well. Buzz has really improved his skills in this area because of those experiences." Greta looked through her phone contacts for Buzz Hill's number. She wrote the number on one of her business cards and handed it to Troy.

"That's a good recommendation." Troy said.

"I think you also might want to look at the new job competencies profile." Greta continued, "If these are the competencies we believe make a sales representative successful here at Mareno, it makes sense to look for evidence of these competencies in job candidates."

"Where do I get potential candidates?" Troy asked.

"Good question." Greta answered. "Sam would tell you that you have to be recruiting all the time and he's right. The best candidates are usually people that aren't looking for a job but rather people that are doing great in their current role. Some might be working for a competitive company. Others might be sales people from other industries. It's even possible that someone who has never sold has such a strong sales aptitude that we might take a chance on them. The point is we have to be looking for top talent all the time."

"I can see that, Greta." Troy said, "But that doesn't exactly help me now. Where am I going to find candidates right now?"

"We can help some in human resources." Greta said, "We may have some active candidates in file. We can also post the position on the Mareno Biosciences website as well as with some of the major on-line services. "

As Troy listened he hoped that these sources would help but also recognized that he needed to do more. He was anxious to talk to Buzz.

"Do you know what you can ask a candidate?" Greta inquired, "In other words do you know how to navigate interviews and stay within the law?"

"I'm not sure about all of the details." Troy said tentatively.

"Fair enough." Greta said, "Please don't interview anyone until you've gone through the on-line training module called <u>Manager and The Law.</u> I'll have Maria, our HR admin assistant enroll you right away."

"That sounds good." Troy said, "Do you have any other modules that could help me?"

"Unfortunately, we don't." Greta answered, "We've been talking for the last couple of years about building a management development library, but we haven't had time to get this done yet."

"What about management training?" Troy asked.

"We are putting on a two-day seminar for people with direct reports before the end of the year. You will be invited. Still, it's pretty general content." Greta answered, "The truth is that most of your training is on the job. That's why I love the way you've been reaching out to your peers. That's the best way to learn at Mareno."

"You said earlier that I should look closely at the competency profiles to prepare for interviewing candidates." Troy asked, "How does that work?"

"Well you turn the competency area into the trait that makes the competency a reality." Greta answered. "I know that sounds confusing. Think about it like this. What trait allows someone to be great at relationship management?"

"Interpersonal skills?" Troy answered.

"That's exactly what I'm talking about." Greta answered, "When interviewing people, you look for evidence of strong interpersonal skills."

"That makes sense." Troy said.

Greta looked at her phone and realized that she needed to get across the street to the airport to catch her flight.

"I'm sorry, Troy." Greta said, "But I'm going to have to get moving. I'll call Maria and get the postings started and get you enrolled in <u>Manager and The Law.</u> In the meantime, if there is anything I can do, please call me. Okay?"

Troy walked down to the lobby with Greta where she could catch the shuttle to the airport.

"Greta." Troy said, "Thank you for all you've done for me. Thanks especially for being here yesterday. I truly appreciate you."

"Always remember." Greta said with a smile, "HR is your friend."

Troy was disappointed that Greta couldn't provide more insights. As soon as she boarded the shuttle, Troy called Buzz Hill.

The phone rang a few times before Buzz answered.

"Buzz Hill." Buzz answered.

"Buzz?" Troy said, "This is Troy Noble."

"Oh, the new guy in the southeast" Buzz said, "How are you doing, bud? Crazy at first, isn't it?"

"Definitely." Troy answered.

"Still drinking from the firehose?" Buzz laughed.

Troy hadn't ever heard that expression but thought it reflected some truth.

"That's one way to put it." Troy answered.

"My friend." Buzz said warmly, "Is this a social call or do you need some help with a crisis?"

Troy laughed, "I need some expertise around hiring people. I was talking to Greta and she said you were the expert."

"Expert?" Buzz laughed, "Or the guy whose made enough bad hires to be a case study on what not to do?"

"She said you could help." Troy answered.

"You're a real diplomat, Troy." Buzz said with a laugh.

"Do you have some time to go through some things with me?" Troy asked.

"Where are you right now?" Buzz asked.

"Across from Atlanta-Hartsfield. Why?" Troy asked.

"Believe it or not, I'm actually stuck here in Atlanta." Buzz answered, "I was headed to Vegas for the American Hospital Administrator's annual meeting and my flight was diverted from Charlotte last night. Now they say they can't get me on another flight until evening. They should be arrested for impersonating an airline. I'm stuck here until tonight. If you're right here in Atlanta why don't you come over to the airport? We can probably meet in one of the conference rooms at the Delta Crown Room."

Troy couldn't believe his good fortune. He drove across to the airport and took the shuttle over to the main terminal. Buzz was waiting in the Delta Crown Room.

Troy immediately knew why the nickname, Buzz was appropriate. Buzz had a flat-top hair cut reminiscent of the 1960s. Buzz, who looked to be in his late forties or early fifties, was about 5'9 and weighed in at around 200 pounds. His frame was covered with a blue and white striped golf shirt with a shark emblem over a pair of Dockers pants.

Buzz reached out his arm and Troy wasn't sure whether he was about to get a handshake or a bear hug.

"Nice to meet you in person." Buzz said as he pumped a hearty handshake.

"Same here." Troy said.

"Let's go get an early lunch." Buzz said, "I'm starving."

Buzz and Troy walked to the center terminal where there was a surprisingly good barbeque restaurant.

"I love this place." Buzz said, "I grew up in Tennessee and everyone knows you can't get good barbeque up north."

"Where do you live?' Troy asked.

"Philadelphia area. My office is in Newtown." Buzz answered, "Nice place, but I envy you living in the south."

"How did you get to Moreno anyway?" Troy asked.

"Funny story. I had been selling endoscopy products for eleven years when I met Sam on a four-hour plane trip from Nashville. My wife and I were headed to Los Angeles to catch another flight to Hawaii on my company award's trip. I was sitting across the aisle from Sam in first class and struck up a conversation before take-off. By the time we landed in LA, Sam had offered me a job at Mareno Biosciences. This was back when Mareno was early in its operation. I came to work at Mareno as soon as I returned from Maui. From the beginning, Sam was lobbying me to go into management and I finally took the plunge after five years as a rep. Three years ago, I accepted the mid-atlantic region job.".

Buzz finally pushed back his plate after telling his story and said, "Well, why don't we go back to the airline club and see if we can't talk through some of what you want to know about recruiting?"

As they walked to the airline club Troy observed, "The way Sam hired you was the same way he promoted me. How does he do that? What do you think he's looking for that allows him to make such quick decisions about people?"

"I have no idea." Buzz answered, "He seems to have a real instinct about it. He goes on gut feeling. A lot of managers do."

"I don't feel confident about making decisions that way." Troy said quietly.

"That's a good thing." Buzz answered laughing, "Believe me, I know. I went on nothing but gut when I first came into this job and did I ever hire a couple of stinkers."

"You don't go on gut anymore?" Troy asked.

"Look, you can never ignore your gut." Buzz answered, "But unless you're blessed with intuition like Sam, you better have a formula for success that goes way beyond gut feelings."

"You have such a formula?" Troy asked as they arrived at the Delta Crown Room.

"Let's go into the conference room." Buzz said, "I'll show you what I do to increase my chances of success."

The two entered a small conference room on the second floor of the airline club. At mid-day, the club was relatively quiet and the conference room the perfect environment for quiet conversation.

"From my experience," Buzz began "You have to know exactly what you're looking for and then find candidates that have already demonstrated success in those areas."

"That's it?' Troy said not meaning to be disrespectful but surprised at such a simple formula.

"That's a lot." Buzz answered. "What do you think a sales representative needs to be successful here?"

"The four areas in the competency model." Troy said, "You know; Relationship Management, Territory Management, Product/Market knowledge and Selling Skills."

"Sure." Buzz acknowledged, "That's a great place to start."

"How were you on those things in your very first job?" Buzz asked.

"You mean my first sales job?" Troy clarified.

"No, I mean your very first job." Buzz said.

"Like, as a busboy at Bob Evan's at 15 years old?' Troy asked.

"Yes." Buzz said with a smile, "As a busboy."

"I wouldn't have even known what those four things were." Troy said laughing.

"Exactly." Buzz said. "But I bet that you were already demonstrating interpersonal skills; you were already showing good organizational and prioritization skills. I bet you could tell people clearly what was on the menu. You may have even begun understanding how to persuade others. Did you ever ask for a raise?"

Troy laughed, "Absolutely. I planned for days exactly what words I was going to say, when my boss might be most receptive, the whole nine yards."

"Did you get the raise?" Buzz said with a grin.

"Yes." Troy answered.

"That, my friend, is evidence that you demonstrated persuasion; what we call selling skills." Buzz said. "And I will bet that you have examples that are similar in every job you've had since."

"But everyone could claim that they were able to persuade someone of something." Troy observed.

"Sure." Buzz said, "But people that really have strong persuasive skills can easily provide situation after situation where they excelled and got results. The better and more numerous the examples, the higher the candidate rates on that skill area."

"You score the candidates that you interview on each of the four areas?" Troy asked.

"Absolutely." Buzz answered, "But I'm not scoring on what candidates say they can do, I score on what they can demonstrate that they've already done."

"How does one account for someone's potential?" Troy asked.

"Potential means they haven't done anything yet." Buzz laughed, "I'd rather let someone else bet on potential. Once there are results, though, I'm all ears."

"But then doesn't that reinforce the old frustration that everyone says they want experience, but no one gives the chance to get it?" Troy asked.

"Not at all." Buzz answered, "I've hired sales representatives without sales experience, but I would never hire someone that couldn't demonstrate persuasion, interpersonal skills, intellectual ability and organizational skills."

"Those are the four areas you score?" Troy asked.

"Yes." Buzz answered, "Every candidate I interview I rate on a scale of 1-10; one being absolutely clueless and ten being the best I've ever seen. This helps me make decisions without being overly influenced by the halo effect."

"The Halo Effect?" Troy asked.

"Sure, we've all been there." Buzz answered, "Somewhere in the conversation the other person says something we agree with so completely that we suddenly feel great about the person. We stop listening objectively because the person now has a 'halo'."

"I think the psychologists call that confirmation bias." Troy said.

"We're one of those prep school academics, are we?" Buzz said with a laugh.

"Yeah, I suppose. I get the concept though." Troy said, "That happens on the negative side too, doesn't it?"

"Sure, but I'm less concerned about that." Buzz observed.

"Why do you say that?" Troy asked, "Couldn't we miss someone really good if we make a decision based on one bad thing they said?

"Sure." Buzz said, "But think of it this way. The interview is the best the candidate is ever going to look. This is where they are putting their best foot forward. They're thinking about everything they say. They probably spent time grooming themselves and picking out what they think is appropriate to wear. They're working hard to show you their best and hide their worst. If something is said that you feel is a red flag, listen and listen closely. Whatever ugliness is there will likely turn into something monstrous when the interview is over and real life begins."

"I guess I can see that." Troy said.

"It even applies to little things to some extent." Buzz said, "One time in the interview process one of the candidates would end every statement with 'see what I mean'?" Now it was a minor irritation during the interview but otherwise the candidate was good. I hired her. Now at the end of a field day with her I am ready to pull out what little hair I have. See what I mean?"

Troy and Buzz both laughed out loud.

"You rate candidates on the four attributes based on their ability to demonstrate evidence of those skill areas." Troy restated, "Does the top score always get the job?"

"That is an excellent question." Buzz said, "Not always"

Troy teased, "You have a system, but you don't always follow it?"

"No, that's not quite true." Buzz said seriously, "There's a bit more to the system."

"I'm listening." Troy said with a smile.

"Even when you have a system to be objective you have to recognize that you aren't immune to subjectivity." Buzz shared. "You have to make adjustments for your own biases."

"Okay." Troy said cautiously.

"Let me give you an example." Buzz said, "I know I'm in trouble during an interview the moment I say to myself, 'he reminds me of me when I was starting out.'"

"I've heard lots of people say that." Troy observed.

"Yes. And that's dangerous." Buzz said, "Because in saying that I am projecting my own successes on to the candidate."

"But isn't that just another aspect to the halo effect?" Troy asked.

"Yes, I think it is." Buzz answered, "But we have to be aware that there are special biases that we have to people that look, talk and act like us. Have you ever seen sales teams where everyone has the same social style?"

"Yes." Troy said, "I've seen that many times."

"With everyone the same, how can a team come up with the diversity of thought necessary for great strategy development and creative execution?" Buzz said.

"True." Troy said, "I remember a college professor once saying that if two people agree on everything one of them is unnecessary."

"I like that." Buzz said, "Sometimes, as the leader you have to think about what is missing from the composition of your group. Do you need cultural diversity? Do you have all four of the basic social styles covered? Do you have people that bring different work experiences to the group? Do you have people of different generations? There is no such thing as the perfect hiring profile. Never compromise on skills but remember that a team works best when different members bring fresh perspectives."

"When you say that the top scoring candidate doesn't always get the job, are you saying that you're considering the team composition?" Troy asked.

"Exactly." Buzz answered, "I select the highest scoring candidate that is the best fit for the team. By the way, I don't only rely on my own judgment with hiring decisions."

"Who else do you involve?" Troy asked.

"It depends." Buzz answered, "But usually one or two of the more trusted members of the region and often one of the other regional managers. Sometimes, Greta will help if she has time. Having each person use the same scoring mechanism helps me compare candidates and usually results in a better decision. I try to provide what I call "five points of contact" before finalizing a hiring decision. This might include a phone discussion, a couple of interviews that I conduct, maybe a day in the field and/or interviews with other members of the team or another regional manager. I don't always get this accomplished, but it is something I shoot for. Certainly, this process is far better than relying on gut feeling."

"You do five interviews?" Troy confirmed.

"Not exactly." Buzz answered, "There are five points of contact but each one is slightly different in what it is trying to achieve."

"What do you mean?" Troy asked.

"Well, a phone discussion allows you to cover a lot of candidates that look good on paper to determine if you want to take the time for a full face-to-face interview. I usually keep these phone discussions to 15-20 minutes. In many companies, these are conducted by HR but here it's pretty much up to us to either do it or delegate it to someone we've prepared for the task. I'm looking for communication skills and interpersonal skills on these calls. It also allows me to confirm any information that might not be perfectly clear on the resume. It is amazing how much you can glean about a person from a few minutes on the phone." Buzz outlined.

"That makes sense." Troy observed, "How many phone screens progress to a face to face interview?"

"First, try not to call them phone screens." Buzz said, "While it's true that we are screening out candidates if you looked at it from the candidate's perspective that doesn't sound very appealing. Sometimes we have to think of things from the candidate's viewpoint especially if we are trying to attract top talent."

"That makes sense." Troy agreed, "How many phone discussions progress to a face to face interview?"

"There's no formula." Buzz answered, "But, I would say that on average I would still progress one out of four candidates after the phone discussion."

"Wow." Troy said with surprise, "Then phone discussions are a real time-saver."

"Definitely." Buzz agreed.

"What about the first face to face interview?" Troy asked.

"I usually schedule these for somewhere between 30 and 60 minutes. As we already discussed, I'm looking for evidence of success in the four areas of skills. You can easily do this in a short timeframe if you stay on track." Buzz outlined.

"I think some of the interviews I've had over the years have taken far more than that. In fact, I always judged how well I did in the interview by how long the interview lasted." Troy said.

"Longer interviews usually happen when the candidate gets the interviewer talking about himself." Buzz said, "One of the biggest mistakes an interviewer can make. When we find ourselves in that situation we come out of the interview feeling great about the candidate even though we did most of the talking. People that have interviewed for a lot of positions know this trick and use it as often as they can. That's why an interviewer must be disciplined with the structure of the interview. It's okay to answer the candidate's questions but this first interview is primarily for us to get to know the candidate."

"That makes sense." Troy agreed, "But when does the candidate get their questions answered?"

"If the candidate doesn't have sales experience I like to send the candidate out for a field day." Buzz answered, "They get to see what the job really entails and what it takes to be successful. Of course, you want to make sure you send them with the right sales representative; someone that understands our legal employment requirements and obligations, has a record of success and demonstrates excellent judgment. Someone that is a good advocate of Mareno Biosciences. If the candidate already knows what the job entails, I recommend that they call one or two of our representatives to get a feel for the company. And of course, since at this point I'm pretty sure I'm going to offer the job, I want to make the candidate feel as special as possible. One way to do that is by being as transparent as possible."

"Does the sales representative also weigh in on the candidate?" Troy asked.

"Absolutely. The candidate often relaxes with the sale representative not understanding that even though informal, this too is a kind of interview. Occasionally, the candidate reveals personality traits that might not come out in a formal interview. Remember though, that you have to coach any such sales representative on your four criteria if you want valuable feedback."

"So, you have a couple of your better sales representatives talk to and assess a serious candidate." Troy confirmed.

"Exactly." Buzz said, "And then I usually do one more final interview that is less structure and more of an equal interaction. This is when we talk about more specific expectations of the job, maybe talk some about the territory and answer any remaining questions the candidate might have."

"Do you give the candidate an offer in this interview?" Troy asked.

"That's a great question." Buzz answered, "I certainly did that earlier in my tenure as a regional manager. Truth is, I gave job offers even earlier in the process. The thing is the more I learned the more about hiring, the more I wanted to be sure about the person I was hiring. There's an old expression that says, 'hire in haste, repent at leisure'. I've lived that."

"You don't offer the job yet?' Troy asked still confused

"Not always." Buzz said, "During this last step of the process I often have one of the other regional managers or Greta present. It's only a confirmation but it helps me to make sure I haven't invested so much in a candidate that I become blind to any red flags. We often then confer and then I extend the offer."

"Have you ever changed your mind after someone else does the confirmation interview?" Troy asked.

"Do you really want me to re-live my pain?" Buzz said with a grin. "I have to tell you early in my tenure I really made some bad hiring decisions. I also didn't get to the five points of contact all at once; it evolved. I think it was my fourth vacancy when I found this guy that I was sold on. It was like we were talking about earlier. I did most of the talking in two interviews and I really liked this guy. At that time, I sent him over to Jim Martin to get his confirmation."

"How did that go?" Troy said with a suppressed smile.

"Terrible." Buzz said, "Jim called me and outlined about five reasons why I shouldn't hire the guy. Then he asked me what in the world I saw in the guy?"

"What did you say?" Troy asked.

I told Jim, "I don't know; he seems like a really nice guy." Buzz said.

"What did Jim say?" Troy asked.

"He said: 'He *is* a nice guy. If I saw him in a bar, I'd buy him a beer, but he can't come to work for us'." Buzz said with a laugh. "Now, that's why I like someone else to look at my candidates."

Troy and Buzz had a good laugh. Then Troy asked with a more serious tone.

"Does the confirmation interview have to be done in person?"

"I almost always have the person confirming sit in on my final interview discussion or occasionally let them do a second meeting at the same time. Occasionally I've had them sit in by Skype but to me that looks a little impersonal." Buzz said, "One of the key objectives at this point is to make sure the candidate feels valued and respected. I also think that a solid recruiting process tells the candidate that we are highly selective and that we really care about them. When we extend the offer, they know they are truly wanted, not some warm body to fill a vacancy."

"That's a good perspective." Troy agreed. "Still, it would seem to me that younger people would think the process is overkill. I would think they might think we were either indecisive or that our processes are overly bureaucratic."

"Yeah, I can see that." Buzz acknowledged, "I think we have to think a little differently with each new generation of potential new hires. I always try to explain up front the reasons for my process, but your point is well-taken."

"During these five points of contact, is there anything else you consider in the hiring process other than success in the four areas you're looking for?" Troy asked.

"Definitely." Buzz said, "I look for values, standards and ethics."

"But how do you really get at such things in an interview?" Troy asked.

"I ask." Buzz answered, "I ask what values they hold in highest esteem. Then I ask them for examples when they've demonstrated those values in their day to day lives. This is often something that people have trouble talking about. I often ask them to describe the best and worst boss they've ever had. You'd be surprised at the venom that often comes out of that discussion. I don't fool myself thinking that I'm going to get at the heart of the person's ethics simply by asking a few questions. Still, if I do nothing else I've established the importance of values to me and to Mareno Biosciences. That might cause a shady person to run the other way."

"I can see that." Troy said. "Would you be willing to interview a candidate or two when I'm further in the process?"

"Of course." Buzz said, "We're all in this together. I'm always here for you."

"Great." Troy said, "Now can you tell me about where you get candidates? Greta said she put the postings up on the website and with some recruiting sites, but I don't know what kind of candidates I'll get. Any thoughts?"

"Absolutely." Buzz answered. "First, don't discount the postings. There will be some good candidates. The problem is the pure volume of candidates you will get through those postings. How I deal with the masses of resume's I get through the website postings is to tighten the requirements of what I'm looking for. For example, I might say that I'm looking specifically for 3 years of selling experience in a medical product area. Since you might get virtually hundreds of resumes' through the postings this will limit those who qualify for a more thorough resume review. Also, make sure that whoever screens the resumes looks at educational experience. We don't hire anyone without a four-year degree and we prefer those with a master's. Make sure those without the degree we're looking for are screened out."

"That makes sense." Troy said, "Who does the screening?"

"If it's one of the commercial sites, sometimes they will do it, although they usually do this by key word search and a few resume's will still slip in that don't qualify." Buzz offered with a smile, "For our own site, you'll probably have to get Carol involved. Don't worry. She will totally hate you for it."

"Once you get the resume's screened how do you decide who to interview?" Troy asked.

"First, I'm always very interested in the career objective." Buzz offered, "Many people are just looking for jobs; there's nothing in the career objective that would indicate a passion for what we do. Then, I look for a pattern of success and a logical pathway that would lead them to a position at Mareno.

Have you ever noticed that some people change careers every few years, changes that seem unrelated? To me, that's like thinking you can build a building by pouring foundation upon foundation. At the end, you don't have a building; you have a big concrete block. There must be what I call a 'golden thread' that ties together everything they've done."

"Interesting." Troy said, "I've never thought of it that way."

"I look very carefully at transitions on the resume'." Buzz continued, "What people do during the key transitions in their lives tells an amazing story of their flexibility and adaptability. Our industry is full of change and it is helpful to know someone is resilient."

"Anything else?" Troy asked.

"The resume' is a person's sales piece" Buzz said, "and most are so boring they don't even pique my interest. I look for someone's ability to make their story come alive."

"Wow." Troy said, "I doubt if I would've even gotten an interview with you."

"Maybe." Buzz said, "But do you see that someone who meets these requirements is really worth the interview?"

"Yes." Troy said, "I do get that."

"Well, that's how I make the decision as to who I want to interview." Buzz instructed.

"That makes sense. What should I do beyond the web postings?" Troy asked.

"Well, let me ask you something." Buzz said, "Who knows better than anyone else what it takes to be a great sales representative for Mareno Biosciences?"

"Is this a trick question?" Troy said with a smile.

"Isn't it someone who is already doing a great job as a sales representative for Mareno Biosciences?"

"Yes." Troy said, "I think that's true."

"Then why don't we ask the members of our team to recommend candidates for us to consider?" Buzz asked.

"Don't we have a referral bonus program?" Troy asked.

"Yes. We give a bonus of $3000 for a recommendation" Buzz answered "Yet, do you know how much we paid out last year in the program?"

"I'm guessing not much." Troy answered.

"We paid out one single bonus." Buzz answered.

"That's amazing." Troy said, "I've got to make this a priority for my team since I now have three vacancies."

"Yes." Buzz agreed, "When a person recommends someone they have skin in the game to ensure that the new person is successful. When a whole region makes this a priority the quality of candidates usually increases significantly. It's not without work on your part, though. Everything you learn about selection standards you must teach to your team. In time, this is a great strategy for recruiting."

"Thanks for sharing that idea." Troy said, "I had forgotten all about the recruiting bonus."

"There's something else you might want to consider. Do you use Linked In?" Buzz asked.

"Doesn't everyone?" Troy asked.

"You'd be surprised." Buzz answered, "Anyway, I regularly go through my on-line contacts and reach out to those who are well-connected and who might know of really good candidates in the specific geographies that I have open. I've found several good candidates this way. I also reach out to sales representatives I know with other companies if I think they might have interest."

"I would think you have to be pretty discrete." Troy said.

"Absolutely." Buzz acknowledged, "I never put anything in Linked In messages about the specific opportunity but rather send out a note to catch up live. I also click on contact information where there is often a private email address. I prefer to use these as contact addresses rather than company email. Don't forget that Linked In is one of the electronic services we use for job postings, as well."

"That makes sense." Troy said, "Anything else?"

"I regularly go through my speed dial contacts on my phone." Buzz said, "Since many people keep their cell numbers over the years, I find I can text people I haven't spoken to for a while and start a dialogue about opportunities or about the desire to catch up live."

"I haven't done that for a while." Troy said, "Good suggestion."

"The thing is you have to be on the lookout for great talent all the time." Buzz said, "I wouldn't necessarily recommend doing what Sam did when he hired me, but getting into recruiting conversations is a solid idea. I've met many people traveling that were successful, sharp and open to new opportunities."

"I will definitely keep that in mind." Troy said, "I travel enough to meet some potential candidates; that's for sure."

"What I'm going to suggest is almost impossible to implement, but you might want to think about it." Buzz said, "Try to have someone you know that is interested in coming to work for us in every single geography that you anticipate could become vacant."

"In my world, that probably means all twelve." Troy laughed.

"That's true of all of us." Buzz said, "But you will find that there are some that become predictable. You will have a couple of sales representatives that are struggling with performance, maybe one or two that are promotable, maybe a couple that are going through big personal transitions in their lives such as marriage, having a child or having to manage care for a parent. It doesn't take a Rhodes Scholar to recognize that these are conditions that could precipitate a vacancy. If you want to maintain a great team, try to have great candidates waiting in the wings".

"That sounds like a big ask." Troy said.

"It definitely is easier said than done." Buzz said "But it is that little competitive advantage that can make all the difference. You know, I have three territories that make up over half of my total sales volume. What do you think happens to team performance when I have a vacancy in one of those geographies?"

"Good point." Troy said, suddenly remembering that in the southeast only four territories compose 60% of the total business.

Troy looked at his phone and recognized that Buzz's flight was scheduled to leave in less than an hour.

"Buzz, thank you for helping me today." Troy said, "This has been helpful."

"You're welcome." Buzz answered, "Recruiting and selection is hard work, but it pays off in a big way and very few people are good at it."

"I know you're right." Troy said putting his iPad back in his briefcase. "Do you remember the kinds of questions we were asked when we were college students on campus interviewing for our first real jobs?'

"As I recall, those interviews were pretty bad." Buzz said with a laugh.

"Yes. I remember being asked why I wanted to go into sales." Troy said.

"Sure. And let me guess your answer…" Buzz said, "Because I'm a people person."

Troy laughed. "That was exactly my answer. This old guy that was interviewing me looked me straight in the eye and said something I've never forgotten."

"What did he say?" Buzz asked.

"He said have you ever considered being a toll booth operator, you'll meet a lot of people in that job." Troy said laughing.

"I guess he'd heard that answer one too many times." Buzz laughed.

"Hopefully, I'll be a little bit more compassionate in my recruiting." Troy said.

"I don't know." Buzz said, "Call me after your hundredth interview."

"Once again, Buzz." Troy said shaking Buzz hand, "Thanks for your help."

"Good luck to you Troy." Buzz answered. "Be careful with your first few hires. The entire southeast team will be watching closely to see how you make decisions. Hiring decisions can define your standards. I'm sure with all we've talked about, you'll do fine."

QUESTIONS TO CONSIDER

1) What role did "gut feeling" have in your being hired?

2) What criteria do you use to evaluate candidates?

3) Which of your direct reports is most vulnerable to resign or leave?

4) What mechanisms do you use for ongoing recruiting?

5) Does your company offer recruiting bonuses?

6) Who do you trust to confirm your hiring decisions? Do you have "5 points of contact"?

7) What personal biases do you have that might keep you from making better hiring decisions?

CHAPTER NINE: OBSERVING THE STARS

Troy drove back to the hotel in time for a light dinner and a quick phone call to Heather.

She answered immediately.

"Troy." Heather said, "I was getting worried about you. You haven't called for two days and you haven't even answered my text messages."

"Oh, I'm sorry, Babe." Troy said, "I had the chance to meet with one of the other regional managers here at the Atlanta airport and my battery ran out. Is everything okay?"

"Sure, but can you try to stay in touch?' Heather said with a mix of hurt and irritation. "I mean, I feel like you're leaving me to do everything with this move. Today, the mortgage company called with all these questions that only you can answer. I know you're busy but I'm trying to close out my job at the hospital, get things ready for the move and deal with Mom and Dad. Mom is acting like we're making this move to get away from them or something. I can handle everything but it's not easy, you know?"

Troy tried to be supportive but while he was listening he was thinking to himself, "Can't she hold this together? I'm working my tail off right now. I don't need all of this." Then, almost immediately he felt ashamed to be so selfish. He realized that the move was weighing heavily on Heather and that she had far more than her fair share of the burden associated with the move. Troy knew that he was letting the job take too big of a role in his life, yet he wasn't sure how to do things differently.

"Baby, I know this is rough on you." Troy said, "Can you email me the name of the mortgage company contact? I'll take care of that tomorrow. I know the information they need is probably on my computer. Your Mom is naturally upset that we're moving but she will calm down in time. And don't worry over all the details of the move. Let me know what you need me to handle. I know you have more than your fair share of the burden of all this."

"You're right." Heather said more with acquiescence than with real confidence. "At least you'll be coming home this weekend, right?"

"Sure. I can come home." Troy said tentatively, "I mean, unless you'd rather come down here to Atlanta. I was thinking maybe we could have a nice weekend together down here, maybe like a mini-vacation."

"Troy, you don't get it." Heather said, the pitch of her voice elevating. "I had to take off work when we did the house hunting trip. I work again Monday morning. I can't walk away from my responsibilities. Even if I could come there and be back on Sunday night I'd be exhausted when I returned, and the house will be a mess. I'll have laundry to do. Look, if you don't want to come home, then fine, stay in Atlanta but I'm not getting on a plane."

Troy began to understand that Heather was overwhelmed. "Babe, no worries." Troy said. "You're right. I wasn't thinking. I'll tell you what. Not only will I come home to Cleveland for the weekend, but I'll come home Thursday afternoon so that we can have more time together."

Heather sounded as though she had regained her composure. "That would be great, Troy." she said, "I know you are under a lot of stress, too. Thanks for understanding."

The rest of the conversation seemed back to normal. Finally, Troy closed the call.

"I love you, you know?" Troy said.

"Baby, I love you too." Heather answered.

"We'll get through all of this, okay?" Troy said.

"I know we will." Heather answered, "Sweet dreams, Baby."

Troy lay down on the hotel bed and starred at the ceiling. He thought of Heather. He thought about the long but productive day at the airport with Buzz. Then he began to think of all he needed to do when he got into regional office the next day. Troy didn't even undress. He fell asleep and didn't wake up until the break of daylight at 6am.

Troy walked over to the hotel window and looked out at the early morning clouds gathering in the west. It looked like the weather forecast had been correct. It would be a rainy day.

Troy showered, changed and grabbed a cup of watery coffee from the hotel lobby before briskly walking to his rental car to head to the office. Troy had thought he would beat the rain since it was only a five-minute drive, but it began to pour before Troy could arrive at the office complex. With no umbrella in the car, Troy ran from the parking lot to the front door of the building, his clothes damp but not soaked from the rain shower.

Harry, the night security guard Troy had met on his very first visit to the office, was still at his station waiting for the shift change that would take place at 7:30.

"You're in here early this morning." Harry said.

"Yeah." Troy said as he waited for the elevator, "A busy day ahead."

"Aren't they all, my friend?' Harry asked with a smile.

Troy unlocked the office and immediately went to start the coffee. He was anxious to have a real cup of coffee in contrast to that offered at the hotel.

He hadn't even walked back to his office when the phone began to ring. Troy thought, "Who would be calling the regional office before 7:30am? Troy picked up the phone.

"Mareno Biosciences, Troy Noble." Troy said.

"Troy." Sam Logan said loudly, "I figured you'd be already up and at 'em. How are things going?"

"Sam. Great to hear from you." Troy said genuinely, "Things are going pretty well, actually."

"Troy, you're really making a good impression on people thus far." Sam complimented, "I heard great things about how you handled the 'come to Jesus' meeting with your team. I think you really got the team on board."

"Thanks." Troy said, "I have a lot of work to do, though. With the vacancies, I'm really going to find it hard to balance everything. I haven't even been in the field yet."

"Yeah, yeah." Sam said, "You'll get everything handled. I'm quite confident. Speaking of vacancies, I've got you covered on one of them. The one in north Georgia."

"Really?" Troy asked, "What do you mean?"

"I sent you over a resume' a few minutes ago. Racheal Hagerty. Wow. What a great family. I worked with Racheal's dad over at Great Plains Health before I came over here. He was a superstar. Bloodline is everything, my friend."

"What's her background?" Troy asked.

"She got her MBA at Duke." Sam said. "I've been wanting to bring a couple of Dukies on board for some time."

"Does she have sales experience?" Troy asked cautiously.

"No." Sam said, "Doesn't need it. Sharp as can be. It's time we shake things up by bringing in a few people with non-traditional backgrounds. Anyway, you look at her. Of course, it's your choice but if I were you I wouldn't pass up an opportunity like this."

"Okay." Troy answered.

"Everything else going well?" Sam asked.

"Yes. So far, so good." Troy said, still thinking about Racheal and the interview process he learned yesterday."

"Good." Sam said, "And Heather? Is she doing okay?"

"Yes, she's fine." Troy answered tentatively thinking about his conversation the night before.

"That's great." Sam said, "If you need anything, you know where I am."

"Thanks Sam." Troy answered.

"Okay. Have a great day." Sam said as he hung up the phone.

Troy had gotten off the phone when Carol arrived at the office.

"Wow, Carol." Troy said, "You get in this early every day?"

"No. Don't get used to it." She said with a smile. "Seriously, sometimes I get in early to avoid Atlanta traffic. GA 400 can be a killer if you wait until rush hour is full blast."

"I just got off the phone with Sam." Troy said, "He says he has a candidate for the North GA vacancy."

"When do they start?" Carol said with a laugh.

"I haven't even looked at her yet." Troy said, "Yesterday, Buzz took me through a pretty extensive recruiting process."

"Yeah, that's for all the regular candidates." Carol said laughing, "When Sam sends somebody; it's a lot easier for everyone if you go through the minimum process necessary and give them an offer."

"Are you saying Sam would be mad if I decided not to hire her?" Troy asked with genuine concern.

"Do you want to be the guy to find out?" She answered. "Besides, don't you have enough on your plate without fighting this battle?'

"Probably." Troy said, "I need to start getting out in the field. Can you start scheduling field days for next week?"

"Sure." Carol said, "Why don't you start in the Atlanta area to make it a little easier on yourself."

"Good idea." Troy said, "Oh yeah. Also, can you get me a flight home to Cleveland Thursday afternoon? I need to keep things running smoothly at home."

"Got it." Carol said, "Heather is getting overwhelmed, huh? That always happens at some point. Be supportive and understanding. It's a lot harder on the spouse than anybody thinks."

"Thanks Carol." Troy said, "I appreciate your understanding."

Troy's cell phone rang. The caller ID read "Dennis".

"Dennis, my friend." Troy said when he answered, "How are you?"

"More importantly, how are you?' Dennis asked.

"I'm doing pretty well." Troy said, "One thing at a time, you know?"

"Yes. I definitely know." Dennis said. "Have you been in the field yet?'

"I start next week." Troy said, "I'm a bit nervous about it."

"Yeah, it can be a little intimidating, at first." Dennis said. "What do you see as your role when you work in the field?"

"Well, I guess I'm there to help people get better." Troy said, "You know, see what they're doing and what it would take to improve."

"You're talking about critiquing what they do and providing suggestions on how to do it better?' Dennis asked.

"Yes, I think so." Troy said, "That's what my bosses have always done for me."

"Fair enough." Dennis said. "Let me ask you a question. Does Heather ever criticize you?

"Sometimes." Troy said cautiously, "Why?"

"When she criticizes you, how well do you take her criticism?" Dennis asked.

Troy laughed.

"That's what I thought." Dennis said with a laugh. "You're telling me that when the person you love more than anyone else in the world, the person who knows you best and that only wants the absolute best for you criticizes you, it is hard for you to accept that criticism?"

"Sometimes." Troy said laughing.

"Then please tell why someone you have recently met, someone who is still nervous having you as a boss would be ready and anxious to hear your golden words of wisdom?" Dennis asked.

"I hadn't thought of it that way." Troy said contemplating what Dennis said.

"Let me give you an alternative plan." Dennis said.

"Okay." Troy said smiling, "I'm all ears."

"The first time you work with any of your new team members look for every good thing that they do and recognize it." Dennis said.

"You mean balance any criticism with positive reinforcement?" Troy asked.

"No." Dennis said, "I mean ONLY provide positive reinforcement. You will have your entire future as a manager to coach weaknesses. For the first time or two I want you to ONLY look for what each person is doing right."

"What if someone isn't doing anything right?" Troy asked.

"Even a stopped clock is right twice a day." Dennis said with a chuckle.

"But when will I get to start coaching the weaknesses?" Troy asked.

"When you're invited." Dennis answered. "Think about it. When you point out everything someone does right they will be surprised. Shocked and pleasantly surprised. You will be building your relationship. Eventually, while all of us appreciate hearing the positive we also naturally will want to find areas to improve. I promise you every single person will eventually say, 'thank you Troy but what do I need to do differently?'"

"And then I can criticize." Troy said.

"No." Dennis said laughing, "Then you say something like. You know, I must think about that. You do many things well, but I'll continue to observe and if I see anything that would really make a difference we can talk about it next time we work together."

"Wow." Troy said, "That's rich. I wish some boss would have treated me that way."

"Well, something to think about Troy." Dennis said.

Troy said, "Thanks, Dennis.

"What coaching methodology do you think you'll use?" Dennis asked.

"I don't know what you mean." Troy answered.

"Well, to be an effective coach, you will probably need a coaching structure so that you can really help your team. We don't have an official one that we've adopted at Mareno. I could recommend someone that could walk you through a solid methodology, though." Dennis suggested.

"Sure." Troy said, "Who do I talk to?"

"There's a guy I know who offers a really simple coaching course called CARE. I think it stands for Coaching and Relationship Essentials. I'll email you his details." Dennis offered.

"Dennis, you've been more helpful than you can even imagine." Troy said, "I was really worried about my work sessions next week but now I can relax knowing all I have to do at the beginning is recognize everything each person is doing right. Thank you."

"No worries." Dennis said, "Always remember, I'm here for you. Oh yeah, one last question."

"I already know what it is." Troy said laughing, "What piece got bigger?"

"Hang in there Troy." Dennis said laughing, "As they say at Disney World, fasten your safety belt, Mr. Toad's Wild Ride is about to begin."

"Talk to you later Dennis." Troy said as he disconnected the call.

When Dennis' email came through with the details of the CARE program, Troy forwarded it to Carol and asked her to schedule him into the next available class.

It was only a few minutes later when Carol came back into Troy's office.

"What is it with you?" Carol said laughing, "Are the business gods watching out for you? There's an introductory CARE class going next Wednesday in Atlanta."

"That's fantastic." Troy said, "Is it expensive?"

"I think your pal Dennis would say it's cheaper than damaging relationships with your team." Carol said with a smile.

"No doubt." Troy said, "Sign me up."

"Already did, Troy." Carol said, "And I've already scheduled your flights for the weekend and your first field days on Monday and Tuesday."

"Now I know why Sam is always bragging about you." Troy said.

The weekend couldn't have been more perfect. Troy's flights were miraculously on time Thursday afternoon and this time there were no notes on the refrigerator when he arrived at the house. Instead, when Troy came in from the garage he was taken aback by his beautiful wife. Heather was dressed in a simple, short, red dress and was made up for an evening out. Heather's almond colored hair had been cut into a chic and sophisticated short style and her stunning brown eyes seemed to sparkle in the early evening sunlight. Troy remembered why and how he fell in love with her nearly ten years prior. He went to her and held her, his heart filling with emotions he had buried with the addictive drive that he had acquired since his promotion.

"Give me a few minutes to shower and change." Troy whispered to Heather, "And then we will go somewhere nice for dinner."

Heather smiled and said, "We have reservations at eight at La Dolce Vita."

Troy grinned realizing that La Dolce Vita was the restaurant where he took her for their very first Valentine's Day dinner together. "What a perfect choice, my Angel." Troy said.

While there were many things swirling through Troy's head regarding Mareno Biosciences he blocked them from his consciousness for this night. He knew that they both needed to talk about other things; memories from their past together and plans for their future."

When they arrived back to their house which would soon also be a memory, Heather leaned over and kissed Troy warmly. "Thank you for being my husband instead of the southeast region manager tonight. I love you and I'm proud of you for your promotion, but it was sweet not to have to compete with the company tonight."

The weekend did allow for discussion of the upcoming move and the many preparations that needed to be made. Still, there was no arguing or dissention. Troy and Heather felt like a team again as they worked through the details together. They discussed Heather's job in Cleveland and some new prospects for her in Atlanta. They talked about the challenges of the move and the opportunities it presented for both. When it was time for Troy to drive to the airport on Sunday there was no division between them, only a sad realization that once again they would be apart for a few days.

Troy's first field day was with Cindy Sherman who covered the Eastern half of Atlanta and nearby suburbs. Cindy had been in her territory for several years although annually realignments had changed some of her geography. Cindy had a pleasant personality and her customers seemed to like her.

Cindy was well-organized in the way she approached her territory, not wasting time driving from place to place. Troy noted that most of the day was spent with nurses and support staff rather than physician and administrative decision makers. Troy also noted that the few interactions he did observe with decision makers were not very persuasive.

Still, Troy buried his critique and instead followed Dennis's formula regarding recognizing the positives.

"You really have a gift with relationships." Troy observed, "It is clear to me that your customers really enjoy seeing you."

"Thanks." Cindy said, "I think that's because I'm not pushy. I've seen some reps hard-sell physicians and I try never to do that."

Troy wanted to comment that maybe that was why Cindy didn't seem to generate a lot of sales, but he kept his thoughts contained.

"Well, I'd say it's because you are a pleasant and respectful person but whatever it is, you should be proud because you probably get in to see some customers that the competition may not."

"Thanks." Cindy said with a smile.

"I also love the way you have organized your territory." Troy said, "You really work an area fully without tons of windshield time. That is good because it helps you get to a lot of customers during your day. This is something many representatives struggle to do."

"Thank you." Cindy said with pride, "I appreciate you recognizing that."

Troy continued throughout the day to recognize every positive thing that Cindy did. By the time they finally pulled into the Starbucks again at 5pm, Troy was exhausted.

"Thanks for a great day, Cindy." Troy said smiling, "I'm really glad we worked together. If the whole team is as strong as you seem to be, we should be able to accomplish a great deal together."

"Thanks, Troy." Cindy said beaming, "I have to admit I was pretty nervous today, but you made me feel comfortable."

"Have a great week." Troy said, exiting Cindy's car.

"You too, Troy." Cindy answered with a smile.

Despite being tired, Troy immediately pulled out his iPad and made a few notes about both the good things he had observed during the work session and some potential areas that might help Cindy at some point in the future.

Troy would have liked to call Dennis to discuss the day, but he only had enough energy left for one phone call. That phone call had to be for Heather.

Troy called Heather and even though the conversation was brief both appreciated hearing the other's voice. Troy had virtually no mental and emotional capacity left when he went to his email and found an advertisement from the gym where he worked out in Cleveland. In big print was the following quotation, "When your mind is tired exercise your body; when your body is tired exercise your mind."

Troy pulled on some gym trunks and t-shirt and went to the hotel fitness center. 45 minutes later after lifting weights he began to feel physically tired but much less stressed. "Good advice from email" Todd whispered quietly, "That has to be a first."

After a good night's sleep Troy was ready for his next field day with Sammy Sherrill.

Unlike the previous day with Cindy, the work session with Sammy Sherrill was a challenge from beginning to end. Sammy had two behaviors that Troy loathed; complaining and bragging. Sammy started complaining about the company before the two of them had even sat down with their first cup of coffee at Panera Bread.

"I cannot understand how this company thinks we will ever become a one-billion-dollar company." Sammy said, "We are such an immature company. And now, we're getting a new product? We can't handle the product we have. I think this company is run by a bunch of clueless chumps sometimes."

Troy realized that he had very little capacity for complaints. He had always worked hard to surround himself with positive people in his social life. Unfortunately, he couldn't make such choices with the team he had been given. Then he thought of something Claudia Jones, his boss at Forbes had once told him.

Troy smiled at Sammy.

"What?" Sammy said, surprised by Troy's calm demeanor.

"I remember having a very similar conversation one time with my old boss at Forbes. I was pointing out how clueless senior management seemed when she told me something I have never forgotten."

"What did she tell you?" Sammy asked.

"She told me that I was holding on to the elephant's tail and describing the elephant as this skinny, curly little thing. She told me to step back and see how much of the elephant I could see. She said that the further back I stood, the more I would see the elephant as a completely different creature." Troy said.

"What's that supposed to mean?" Sammy asked.

"She was pointing out to me that sometimes senior management decisions looked really stupid to me because I was too close to a situation to see the whole picture." Troy answered, "She was telling me that sometimes if I had more information the decisions would look a lot smarter."

"You're telling me I'm nearsighted?" Sammy said wounded.

"Not at all Sammy." Troy said, "I'm only telling you what Claudia told me. From that point on if I started questioning the wisdom of company decisions; she would smile at me and say one thing. Take a step back Troy; how much of the elephant can you see?"

"You're one of those guys that think the company is always right." Sammy said sarcastically.

"No" Troy said calmly, "And I'm not suggesting that you should be either. Companies are always made better by bright people that are willing to think differently. Claudia's little rule helped me know what to challenge over the years."

"Yeah," Sammy said, "Whatever."

Troy knew it was going to be a long day.

"Let's stop talking and get out there and make things happen." Sammy said, "Our product isn't going to sell itself, you know."

Troy remembered Dennis saying to only look for the positive and he wondered if he should have even mentioned the whole elephant story. It seemed like it set Sammy on the defensive. Troy was determined to only look for the good for the rest of the day.

Sammy didn't make this easy. He not only complained continuously but also kept bragging how he had been carrying the entire state of Georgia for some time. He complained that the two representatives that left recently, Marty and Cynthia were cheaters and that Cindy Sherman was "worthless" as a sales representative.

Troy struggled with how to handle this because while he wanted to be positive he also had no desire to reinforce an attitude that was toxic to establishing an effective team. Had the negative comment about Cindy been a single reference, Troy would have let it pass but upon repeated references to "the clueless rep in the next territory" and "miss wonderful but worthless" Troy had heard enough.

"Sammy, when it is safe, please pull the car over to the side of the road." Troy said calmly.

"Why?" Sammy asked almost in a panic. "Is everything okay?"

"Just pull over." Troy said quietly and calmly.

Sammy pulled over into a convenience store parking lot.

"Sammy," Troy began, "I've observed many things that could make you a true asset to the southeast region and I really want to spend our time talking about those things but there's something that I cannot allow any longer."

Sammy looked shocked and concerned.

"I cannot allow any team member to show constant disrespect to another." Troy said seriously, "You have been repeatedly referring to a team mate in a most disrespectful manner. I'm sorry I didn't say something right away, but I am saying it now. I simply don't want to ever hear that again."

"I can't believe you." Sammy said, "I was kidding. Don't you know that sales people kid each other all the time?"

"I'm serious, Sammy." Troy said, "I'm sorry to have this discussion so soon but this is one of those things that is simply non-negotiable. Okay?"

"Sure, boss." Sammy said with venom in his voice, "I'll keep my opinions to myself."

Troy took a deep breath. Sammy pulled back out on the road and the two rode in silence to the next call. This wasn't turning out like Troy had hoped.

Later in the day, Troy tried to outline the many things that Sammy was doing well but Sammy didn't seem to be open to positive reinforcement. Any potential bond of trust seemed severed.

Both Sammy and Troy were glad when the day had ended.

"I'm sorry we didn't get off to a better start." Troy said, "I really am impressed with much of what you bring to the party for us. Your selling skills are strong, and you are very persuasive when sharing clinical data. I'm hoping that we can establish a very good working relationship over time."

"I'm sure things will get better." Sammy said, "Good luck with the rest of your week."

While the work session was finished Troy felt there was little closure to the discomfort of the day.

Troy imagined what the phone conversations must be like between Cindy, Sammy and the other members of the team. From experience, Troy knew how quickly discussions occurred regarding what is was like to work with a new manager. Troy felt that Cindy's conversations and Sammy's would be different as summer and winter.

Troy suddenly thought about the CARE Coaching seminar he would be attending for the next two days. He sure hoped that the upcoming class would give him new tools to better deal with these kinds of situations. In fact, he thought that the success of the team might depend on it.

QUESTIONS TO CONSIDER:

1) How would you handle a candidate referral from senior management?

2) What do you do to "compartmentalize" your time with your family?

3) What would your next steps be with Cindy?

4) Was this first field day the right time and place to confront Sammy?

5) What would you do to repair your relationship with Sammy?

CHAPTER TEN: COACHING THE STARS

The CARE Coaching Seminar was held at the Atlanta Airport Westin, a great location for those flying in from elsewhere but a remote site for someone driving from Alpharetta. Troy had been expecting a large auditorium full of attendees and was surprised that the program was to be conducted in a conference room with only four participants.

The seminar leader, Mike wasted no time in getting into the agenda. It was clear from the beginning that this was not a lecture-like program but rather one that was case-based and highly interactive.

During the icebreaker exercise Troy learned about the other participants. Alexis Adams was a new sales manager for small biotech company that sold a regenerative medicine product. She was 34, had a master's degree in biochemistry and had been the top sales person at her company prior to being offered the management job. She had eight of her former peers now reporting to her.

Eric Denson had been a first line manager for three years at a growing medical device company. Their cutting edge surgical product had grown so quickly that the national sales team was recently increased from ten to sixty sales representatives. As a result, they needed a National Sales Director and five new first line managers. Eric was selected as the National Sales Director and was hoping to use the CARE coaching methodology with his new management team.

Betsy Bains had been a sales manager with a specialty oncology company for two years and had suffered significant turnover. In fact, of her 10 direct reports all but one had resigned. She was required to attend a coaching skills course by her boss. She freely shared with the training group that this was her last chance to "get people management".

Troy explained to the group that he was a new manager and outlined his earlier in the week experiences with Cindy and Sammy. "I'm hoping I find some answers here because I feel pretty lost on how to provide feedback." Troy said.

"I remember the very first exposure that I had to a coaching program," Mike said, "The speaker asked how much productivity was being lost that day because we, the managers of our company were sitting in the seminar? Of course, there were various answers. There was one egomaniac manager who thought that his team's productivity was cut in half because he was out of the field. I think there are good drugs available for those kinds of delusions."

There was mild laughter from the participants.

"Most of us figured that the actual lost sales productivity was pretty minimal. The seminar leader then he asked how much productivity would be lost if we were at work, but our teams were sitting in a seminar" Mike said. "We all got the point. We needed our teams a lot more than they needed us."

Mike stopped to let the point settle.

"The truth is each of us has a true opportunity to make a big difference in the lives of every one of our employees." Mike said, "But before we can do that we need to understand the essence of coaching."

Mike asked the participants to describe their own experiences at being effectively coached.

Eric started, "I used to hate to play golf because I was shockingly bad at the game. There are too many things to remember. Keep your head down, keep your left arm straight, grip the club a certain way, work on your stance, watch your backswing, follow through; I mean I was absolutely overwhelmed."

"I can relate to that." Troy said enthusiastically, "Did someone help you to be better?"

"It was amazing." Eric said, "There was this amateur champion golfer at my church who asked if I wanted to go for a round of golf at her country club. I did my normal 25 things wrong and she didn't say a thing. Five holes into the round of golf she finally asked permission to make a suggestion. Of course, I wanted to hear what she had to say."

"What was her big tip?" Betsy asked.

"She told me to swing the club like it was an elephant's trunk." Eric laughed, "Exactly like you pretend to do with your arms when you're in kindergarten. I did it repeatedly. I felt like a fool. Finally, after I had a perfectly smooth elephant's trunk swing back and forth she teed up a golf ball and told me to hit it with that same swing. It was the first time I hit a ball solidly. The thing soared."

"And now you're a star golfer?" Alexis asked.

Eric laughed, "Don't I wish. But that one thing I've never forgotten. It really made a difference."

Mike spoke up, "In CARE we call that coaching the right WHAT"

"What?" Betsy asked.

"Exactly." Mike answered.

Everyone laughed as the conversation was beginning to sound like an Abbott and Costello routine.

"Seriously," Mike noted, "The very first thing that you have to do as a coach is to understand what is worth coaching. When we get into the specifics of the CARE methodology we will spend a lot of time on this. For now, though let's hear some other coaching successes. Betsy, how about you?"

"It's funny you ask." Betsy answered, "When I was a new sales representative I was really good in front of the customer. I was selling a ton of product. One thing I didn't like to do was weekly reports. I thought they were a total waste of time. Honestly, I didn't always do them and when I did they were always late."

"Any of you have sales people like that?" Mike asked with a grin.

Everyone was shaking their heads in agreement.

"You were coached on this issue?" Mike asked Betsy.

"My old manager put up with it." Betsy said, "But then this new manager comes in. He first told me what I great sales person he thought I was and how excited he was to have me on his team. Then he told me that he heard that I was often late on reports."

"Gotcha." Alexis said with a laugh.

"Exactly." Betsy continued, "I joked about it telling him that I loved making things happen and that paperwork was a low priority for me. He smiled at me and said that he was almost sure that in the coming year I wouldn't be late on a single report. I asked him how he could be so sure. He told me that every time I was late he would deduct $100 from my quarterly bonus. Guess how many times I was late?"

"I bet none." Alexis answered with a laugh.

"Actually, I was late once." Betsy said, "But still I thought that was pretty effective coaching."

"Wow. Another great story." Mike said, "And it illustrates another part of the CARE methodology. You guys are amazing. You're teaching yourselves."

"Great." Troy said, "Then will we get our fees back?'

"A group smart enough to teach themselves already knows the answer to that question." Mike said with a chuckle. "Seriously though, the second part of the CARE methodology is outlining the WHY; in other words, helping the person you're coaching to understand the benefits of change and the consequences of not changing. Betsy's manager clearly identified the WHY. This will be an important part of our program. Anyone have an example of someone simply coaching how to do something better?"

Troy stepped up. "Yes. Recently one of my colleagues took me through exactly how to do a business plan. It was a true step by step instruction that made such a difference for me. I had never seen the value of putting together that kind of plan before. Through his coaching, I learned how to design a plan that truly has become my blueprint for my team's success."

"Did he tell you what to do or coach you to do it yourself?' Mike asked.

"Believe me, if you knew this guy you would know he made me do the work." Troy said thinking of Jim Martin's no-nonsense style.

"The reason I ask is because much of the time managers really miss the mark on the HOW step of coaching." Mike observed, "Either they leave the employee without a clue as to how to implement change or they want to provide the plan of action themselves in which case there is no real ownership. We will learn today how to do the HOW."

"What?' Alexis said in a kidding manner.

"No, How." Mike said laughing; picking up on spirit of the Abbott and Costello joke.

"It's funny, though." Mike observed, "That each of your experiences with effective coaching had to do with a different element of the CARE methodology. Imagine, how effective you will be when you nail down each of the four steps of the coaching process?"

"Did I miss something?" Betsy asked, "I only remember you mentioning three; WHAT, WHY and HOW."

"Good catch." Mike answered, "The fourth is all about follow up. In the CARE methodology we call that step...WHEN."

"This sounds overly simple." Eric said, "WHAT, WHY, HOW and WHEN. Is that all there is to it?"

"Simple as golf, my friend." Mike said with a laugh. "Simple but definitely not easy."

"Why don't we get started with a real example?" Mike said as he handed out a case study.

Each participant read the case of Patti Pleasant:

The STAR Manager

Patti is an Account Manager with slightly above average sales performance. She has been with the company ten months after a sales career of several years with a pharmaceutical company. While Patti has maintained a "good" job rating she has never had a banner year of sales productivity.

As her new Region Director, you are trying to diagnose her problem. During your observations today, Patti never really has given a selling presentation. In this important wound care center account, she has free access to virtually all her customers, but you have yet to observe a good clinical or business discussion. This morning you have already seen the podiatrist and vascular surgeon working in the wound care center as well as the program director of the center. Dr. Davis seemed open to discussion while discussing the upcoming case but Patti made small talk rather than making a single point about PerfectSkin. When Patti ran into the chief of infectious disease (who is on the inpatient wound care team) at the hospital she handed him a brochure on the elevator and told him, "I don't know how much you know about PerfectSkin but they use it all the time in the wound care center."

Patti then told you that "since he doesn't see patients at the wound care center she didn't want to bore him with the details."

On another call Patti knocked on Dr. Groop's door, asked if he had gotten any baby pictures of his new grandson and then talked for ten minutes about the child's progress at rolling over. Dr. Groop then got up and said he had a case to attend to. Patti briefly asked if the patient was going to get the PerfectSkin she had ordered for the procedure and Dr. Groop asked her if she had time to prepare the graft. Patti sighed but agreed to thaw the product.

On her visit with Dale Derman, the program director of the wound care center, Patti walked in, said she had someone she wanted Dale to meet and then introduced you as "one of the big shots". There was a brief discussion where Patti asked, "So how is everything going with PerfectSkin?" and the director answered, "Things are going fine. No worries." While not ideal, Patti is up 10% in this account while her territory shows flat growth.

Patti mentions PerfectSkin on every call, but there is nothing said that you would consider compelling.

It will soon be the lunch hour and you will have an extended time to talk to Patti about her morning.

Mike asked the team to discuss what is the WHAT? After a few minutes of discussion, the group wrote the following on the flipchart:

What is the WHAT?

-Patti needs to give presentations instead of making social calls

-Patti might not have good enough product knowledge

-Patti inappropriately introduced her boss

-Patti wastes selling opportunities

-Patti's sales are flat

"With several possibilities listed as to potential 'WHATs'" Mike said with a grin, "Which WHAT will you choose to coach?"

The group discussed their ideas about how to prioritize the potential areas for coaching. Finally, Mike handed out a quick reference guide to CARE.

"Look at this Quick Reference Guide because it outlines several qualifiers for the WHAT part of CARE. The rules are straight-forward" Mike said, "In the case of sales representatives the questions are simple:

      Is this the most critical issue at hand?

      If it changes will sales increase?

      Which competency behavior does it reflect?

      Is there a pattern of behavior?

      Is it specific enough to change?

The group looked carefully at the quick reference guide.

WHAT needs to change? 1) Is this the most critical issue at hand? 2) If it changes will sales increase? 3) Which competency behavior does it reflect? 4) Is there a pattern of behavior? 5) Is it specific enough to change? Communication Points: 1) State the behavior clearly and concisely 2) Provide examples 3) Ask the individual for their thoughts	WHAT should be repeated? 1) Is this the behavior most responsible for success? 2) If the behavior is repeated will sales increase? 3) Which competency behavior does it reflect? 4) Is there a pattern of behavior? 5) Is it specific enough to repeat? Communication Points: 1) State the behavior clearly and concisely 2) Provide examples 3) Express appreciation

WHY must it change?
1) Positive Consequences for changing
  - To others
  - To the individual
2) Negative Consequences for not changing
  - To others
  - To the individual
 	
Communication Points:
1) Restate the behavior to change
2) Ask the individual to outline positive consequences of changing
3) Ask the individual to outline negative consequences of not changing
4) Ask "Do you understand why this must change?"
5) Ask "Are you willing to make this change?"
	WHY does it matter?
	1) Value to others
	2) Value to the individual
	
	Communication Points:
	1) Restate the successful behavior
	2) Tell the individual the value the behavior provides to others
	3) Tell the individual the value the behavior provides to themselves
	4) Thank the person for the behavior

HOW will it change? "If you can name it and understand it, you can change it." 1) Propose strategy and tactics 2) Test impact 3) Refine 4) Write it down.	HOW did it come about? "If you can name it and understand it, you can repeat it." 1) Ask how the individual accomplishes the behavior 2) Look for solutions to use with others

WHEN will it change?	WHEN did it become refined?
1) When will change occur? 2) How will we know? 3) Tie consequences to change.	1) How long did it take to refine the behavior?

Alexis was the first to speak out. "By these rules, I guess the real issue is that Patti simply needs to start giving sales presentations. At this point, we know this has to change and sales would increase if she is able to change it."

Eric added, "The problem is we aren't really sure which competency is involved. It could be product knowledge is weak. It might also be that she has poor selling skills."

"Or even some underlying belief that she would offend her customers by trying to give presentations" Betsy added.

"We do see that there is a pattern of behavior." Troy observed.

Mike acknowledged the group. "Great observations." Mike said, "And you're all right. You've identified WHAT needs to change. When you follow the structure of the WHAT discussion you will also likely drill down to the root cause of the behavior you are coaching. You'll note that the three things you do when you discuss the WHAT are:

- State the behavior that needs to change
- Provide examples of the behavior
- Ask the person you're coaching for their thoughts.
-

"Let's try this." Mike said, "Troy can you state the behavior the needs to change?"

"I'll try." Troy said, "Patti, something I've noticed this morning was that you saw many customers but really never got into a selling presentation."

"Good start." Mike said, "What is a selling presentation?"

"Are you kidding?" Troy asked.

"Not at all." Mike said. "Patti may define a selling presentation differently than you."

"Okay." Troy said, "Instead, maybe something like this. Patti, we know that we are most effective when we get into a discussion with the customer about their needs and how our product might meet those needs. In our many calls today, I didn't really see that happening with your customers."

Mike acknowledged, "That is much closer. Betsy, can you provide some examples to Patti?"

"Sure." Betsy said, "Patti, some examples of this are with Dr. Groop when the social discussion about his grandson never transitioned into a sales presentation. And when Dr. Davis seemed open to discussion you made small talk about sports and then later with the Chief of Infectious Disease you simply handed him a brochure and only mentioned the product."

"Good." Mike said, "Now you can see how the more we do this the better we will get at providing feedback in a way others can receive. Eric, now can you ask Patti her thoughts?"

"Sure." Eric said, "I'm curious, what are your thoughts about my observations?"

"Great question." Mike said, "Now you've opened up the topic for discussion. What do you think Patti might say?"

"She'll probably say that this almost never happens; that she does selling presentations almost all the time." Betsy said.

"That might happen." Mike acknowledged, "That's why you need several examples. You want to see a pattern of behavior before you try to change something. What else might she say?"

"Maybe that she wasn't trained." Eric said.

"Or that she is unsure of some of the clinical data." Troy added.

"Or maybe she had something on her mind and was distracted." Betsy said.

"Or that she didn't want to offend her customers." Troy said.

"It really could be almost anything." Alexis said with a sigh.

"Exactly." Mike said enthusiastically, "But do any of these things change your feelings about her need to start giving selling presentations?"

The group all shook their heads in the negative.

"Gaining her perspective isn't going to change the outcome of the coaching interaction," Mike said, "But it might change how you resolve the issue."

"The WHAT step is all about defining the problem." Mike continued, "Once you agree on the WHAT it is time to move to the WHY. WHY is about two things; benefits of changing and consequences of not changing. Most people would rather change because they see benefits as opposed to consequences, but both work. What have each of you changed recently? Was it a result of benefits or consequences?"

"I recently lost 15 pounds." Eric said, "My wife made a comment one night about me gaining a small pot belly. I was devastated. I had always promised myself I wouldn't become one of those guys with a gut. I lost weight and started lifting weights because I wanted to look good again for my wife"

Betsy then said, "I eliminated credit card debt. I noticed that I was giving away money to credit card companies that I could be spending for something else. I added up all the interest I'd paid in two years and it was over $2000. I figured I could go on a great vacation for that."

"What about you, Troy?" Mike asked.

"I took up Spanish." Troy said, "Every time my wife and I traveled to Mexico she could speak the language and I felt stupid. I hate feeling stupid."

Alexis jumped in, "I started reading at least one book per month for a similar reason. I wanted to feel like I was conversant on more topics."

"Good move Alexis." Mike acknowledged, "You know the old expression, 'readers are leaders and leaders are readers'."

Alexis smiled but rolled her eyes.

"Seriously," Mike continued, "These are all great examples of changes initiated with a specific benefit in mind. There are times when we do things to avoid consequences."

"Yeah, I get that because I've got kids." Eric said with a laugh, "If it wasn't for the threat of taking away video games, nothing would get done at my house."

"And you have that luxury as a parent to use threats to a much greater degree than you do in the workplace." Mike observed, "But if done correctly, the employee will often identify consequences for themselves."

"How does that work?" Troy asked.

"Let's go back to the Quick Reference Guide." Mike offered. "According to the guide, who outlines benefits and consequences?"

"The employee?" Alexis asked.

"Exactly." Mike agreed. "Think of our example with Patti Pleasant. Once you've got clarity that Patti must start dialoguing with the customer regarding their needs and how the product might fulfill those needs, you might ask her a question. Anyone want to take a stab at this?"

"Sure." Betsy answered, "I would say Patti, if you were able to give a selling presentation on every call how do you think you would benefit?"

"What might she say?" Mike asked.

"She might say that her sales would improve or that she would feel better about her job." Alexis said.

"Yes." Mike said, "And the benefit of better sales performance might extend to the team and the company too."

"But what happens if Patti is too stubborn to recognize benefits?" Betsy asked.

"What do you think?" Mike returned the question

"Then I guess I would ask her to outline what she thinks will happen to her if she doesn't change." Betsy said tentatively.

"You are absolutely correct." Mike said. "Troy, can you put this into a question for Patti?"

"Patti, I get that you don't see benefit in changing." Troy said, "But this is important to your success. How do you think you'll be impacted if you don't change?"

"That is a great question." Mike observed, "Let me tell you why. An employee will almost always come up with more severe consequence than you would. This allows you to appear conciliatory while getting agreement to change. Let's role play this. Betsy, you be Patti. How would you answer Troy's question?"

"You aren't going to fire me over this are you?" Betsy said overdramatically.

Mike interrupted, "That is such a likely response. If you know you wouldn't fire her over this, what might you then ask?"

Everyone was silent and then Eric spoke up. "I might say something like; No, you probably wouldn't get fired but what else could happen to you?'

"Eric, that is a great question." Mike observed, "Patti then might talk about her bonus being compromised or her performance rating might be lowered. Now, Patti would be seeing the potential consequences without you making a single threatening statement. Once this happens, all you have to ask is; do you see why it is important to start giving selling presentations on every call?"

"That's pretty cool." Alexis observed, "Because of course she is going to agree."

"Yes." Mike said, "And then all you have to ask is if you have her commitment to change. Believe me, at this point the answer is almost always a resounding YES."

The CARE coaching methodology was shaping up to be an easy structure for the group to follow; especially after several case studies and role play simulations.

In the afternoon, Mike introduced the How component of the CARE methodology.

"Once we have agreement and a commitment to change, the real work begins." Mike stated, "How many times have you seen someone commit to a change and then nothing actually changes?"

Everyone's hand went up.

"This happens because a plan with true accountability was never implemented" Mike said, "I once met a smoker who quit twenty-three times. He knew what needed to change; he knew the benefits and consequences. He even committed to the change. The one thing he was missing was a plan of action that would work.

The problem is that most of the time we have already tried everything we know to do...we need fresh perspective and novel solutions. For my friend who smoked, success didn't come until the twenty-third attempt. That is because he finally outlined all the triggers that made him want to smoke and he built strategies for every single one. For example, while at work there was no smoking allowed in the building so smokers had to go outside in the breezeway to light up. They huddled in their winter coats in the snow and wind. Tony had planned this time to succeed so he started having his wife drive him to work and left his coat in the car. Tony knew that there was no way he would go outside in Minneapolis in January without a coat. This kept him from smoking at work. He had similar strategies for every one of his triggers."

"That's impressive." Eric said, "Was that his idea?"

"Great question." Mike answered, "No, the idea was a suggestion from one of his co-workers. In fact, the rest of the plan was completely his, but this one suggestion made all the difference. Which takes us to implementation of coaching the HOW. Let's look once again at the Quick Reference Guide."

The group looked at the guide.

"You'll notice that there is this quotation." Mike said, "If you can name it and you can understand it, you can change it." "What does that mean to you?" Mike asked the group.

"Well, we defined the WHAT already. That is naming it" Alexis observed.

"Yes, and in the WHY we often gain understanding as to why the WHAT happens." Eric added

"The change it part only works if you design a plan that gets to the heart of what causes the problem to start with." Alexis finished.

"Yes." Mike said, "That's pretty much the idea. Let me give you an example. One of my clients told me about a sales representative that talked non-stop. She said that the employee could drive for two hours and never stop talking. She said he was driving her nuts. What do you think my first question was to the manager?"

"Is this the most critical issue to address?" Troy said with a smile.

"Yes, and the following one." Mike answered, "If this changes will sales increase? If her answer had been a solid no I would have told the manager to get over it, but she said that the sales representative was alienating customers because they were overwhelmed by his constant chatter and his interrupting during attempted conversation. As a result, sales were negatively impacted."

"The manager addressed the problem by outlining the WHAT. The manager even got agreement to change by using the benefits and consequences in the WHY step. But no matter what plan of action was put into place nothing seemed to change." Mike continued.

"Was it a lost cause?" Troy asked.

"Not at all." Mike said. "The manager followed the HOW step and together the sales representative and the manager came up with a solution that worked."

"What did they come up with?" Betsy asked.

"First, the manager had the sales representative come up with the steps he thought would work. These included asking friends, family and colleagues to provide a cue of placing their finger on their nose whenever he was dominating the conversation. Secondly, the sales rep thought that if he wrote out the key things he wanted to say before each call that he was more likely to stay on track. He had a couple of other ideas, as well." Mike said, "What does the quick reference guide say to do next?'

"Test the impact." Troy said.

"What do you think that means?" Jim asked.

"I'm not sure." Troy answered.

"Testing the impact means going step by step and asking the question, if you do this will it totally resolve the problem?" Mike said.

"The answer to that question was negative?" Alexis asked.

"Yes." Mike answered, "Because the sales representative wasn't with his friends, family and colleagues during sales calls and writing down what he wanted to say only made him more anxious to get everything said."

Everyone laughed.

"The manager had a practical suggestion." Mike continued, "She suggested that he watch the lips of his customers and if he saw them move at all, he was to stop talking. That is called refinement of the plan."

"Did it work?" Betsy asked.

"Yes." Mike said, "Because it was something practical and kept him from interrupting his customers, it worked. Eventually, the sales representative applied the same technique to social situations as well. It made a true difference in his life."

"Wow." Eric exclaimed.

"Yes." Mike agreed, "Sometimes, it is amazing how much we can help people if we focus on the right things."

"The HOW part of the CARE methodology is to have the employee outline the steps they will take to change, then test those steps for impact, then refine the plan with fresh ideas...anything else?" Betsy asked.

"Only to write it all down." Mike said, "The biggest reason for a lack of change is poor managerial follow up. That will be the focus of the WHEN step of CARE but it starts with writing down the agreed steps during the HOW component."

"Writing key elements of feedback is always a good idea." Mike said, "I'm sure most of your companies have field work session report."

All four participants nodded their heads.

"These documents are great places to put the action steps." Mike said enthusiastically. "The field reports make it possible to show progress over time, allow you to ensure a continuum to your coaching and serve as a great follow up tool for the HOW and WHEN components of the CARE methodology."

"What do you mean by continuum of coaching?" Betsy asked.

"Thanks for asking that." Mike responded, "I like to think of it this way. Every time you work with a sales representative you get a snapshot of their performance. The idea is to put all those snapshots together to make a movie. You want to coach the big, significant issues and those probably won't suddenly resolve themselves in one work session. Looking back on previous field reports and tying those to what you do on your next work session provides a continuum of coaching that will really help you change behavior."

"That makes sense." Betsy acknowledged.

"There is a real need to develop our written documentation to align with verbal feedback. This is important to ensure that everyone is treated fairly and to keep us compliant with laws and regulations." Mike continued, "While we won't be addressing this in detail today, this is a topic on which you will want to get more information. But let's go to the final component of the CARE methodology. What do you think is involved in the WHEN step?"

"This one seems pretty straight forward." Alexis spoke up, "It is confirming a deadline for completion, isn't it?"

"Well, that's an important part of it." Mike answered. "Let's go back and look at the Quick Reference Guide one more time."

The participant's turned their attention to the guide.

"I like to think of three dates in the WHEN step." Mike said. He went to the flipchart and wrote the following:

- **WHEN** will you start?
- **WHEN** do you anticipate results?
- **WHEN** will we know this issue has been resolved?

"Let's take the example again of Tony, the smoker." Mike said, "How would you think Tony would have answered these three questions?"

Eric spoke up. "I'd say he started the next day after he built his plan. Maybe, he would have felt he was beginning to get results if he went three or four days without a cigarette."

"That's exactly the way to look at this." Mike reinforced, "When would Tony know that he was successful quitting cigarettes?"

"Probably, if he went a month without cigarettes he would feel that he kicked the habit, I'd say." Eric said.

"Who comes up with these milestones during a coaching session?" Mike asked

"The employee." Betsy said, "Unless they are really unrealistic, then the manager might help."

"Great point, Betsy." Mike said, "Most of the time, the employee will set pretty aggressive timelines, though."

"You'll note that in the guide it also asks the coach to re-iterate the benefits or consequences in the WHEN step. This is more of a summary than a hammer. The employee simply reminded why the change is important. Now, if you've gone through all the trouble of writing out the HOW and putting dates to the WHEN, what are you going to do next as the manager?" Mike asked.

"Follow up." Eric answered.

"If we all know we should do great follow up," Mike said, "Why is it that managers often fail at this?"

"I know for me, I just forget." Betsy answered.

"I usually try to do follow up on my office day but then get hung up with conference calls and fire drills." Alexis added.

"If I don't put it in my calendar, it doesn't get done." Eric added.

"Yes." Mike acknowledged, "There are many things that keep us from follow through on action plans. Yet, this is the primary reason employees don't accomplish the things that we coach. Have you ever worked hard on something and then your boss acts like she totally forgot the project?"

"Happens all the time." Betsy answered, "And honestly, it really makes me mad."

The others were nodding in agreement.

"Don't be that manager." Mike said, "Nothing shows a lack of respect more than asking someone to change something and then never mentioning it again. Let's put an action plan together for ourselves for follow up. What are you going to do differently?"

"I like Eric's idea of putting follow up on key action points on my Outlook calendar." Betsy said.

"I think reviewing the last field report for each sales representative on every Friday might work." Alexis added.

"I'm going to make sure to load the most recent field report on my iPad so when I have normal day to day phone conversations, I can pull them up and ask about progress on the action steps." Troy added.

"These are great ideas." Mike said, "If you do these three

things will this guarantee that you will follow up with each of your employee's action plans?"

Troy started laughing. "I get it. You're demonstrating the HOW part of coaching on us."

"Guilty as charged." Mike said, "Can I make another suggestion? Might you consider scheduling a brief follow up call every day with a different employee? If you do this on a rotating schedule you can probably even make it a standing time and date, like every other Tuesday at 5:30pm. This added to your other ideas, should pretty much ensure that follow up takes place regularly across your teams. I promise you it will be well worth the effort."

"Please tell me you're not going to demonstrate the WHEN step on us." Betsy said with a groan.

"No, I'll spare you but I'm glad you're taking this all to heart." Mike said with a smile. "It's hard to believe but our time is up for today. Are there any questions?"

"Yes." Troy asked, "Is this all there is to effective coaching?"

"I wish it were so." Mike answered, "This is only a beginning. CARE simply provides some structure to your coaching sessions. There is much to be learned about how to coach people with differing social styles, what to do when it is a 'will' issue as opposed to a 'skill' issue; in fact, there are many aspects of coaching but following the CARE methodology is a very good foundation."

"In other words, you have more programs for us to attend." Eric said laughing.

"It is a journey, my friend." Mike answered.

The workshop had barely ended when Troy pulled out his cell phone and noticed the flashing green light indicating a queue of messages. He quickly glanced at the text messages seeing two from Heather, several from team members and one very urgent message from Sam. Sam's message caught Troy's eye. It simply read, 'CALL ME NOW." It was sent to Troy three hours ago. Troy's stomach began to churn.

QUESTIONS TO CONSIDER:

1) What change do you most need to make in your life?

2) What are the benefits of changing? The consequences of not changing?

3) Who can you ask for fresh ideas for your own action plans?

4) What will you do differently regarding follow up with your direct reports?

5) How do you feel about the "qualifiers" for determining appropriate WHAT's to coach?

6) Are there some situations you might coach that don't fit the rules?

CHAPTER ELEVEN: ASSESSING THE STARS

Troy went out into the hotel lobby and found a relatively quiet spot where he could talk on the cell phone and hear what Sam had to say.

Troy speed-dialed Sam's number and Sam answered immediately.

"Where in the Hell have you been all day?" Sam said with irritation in his voice.

"I was in a coaching seminar today" Troy replied.

` "How much training do you need, Troy?" Sam said loudly, "You could've probably taught that coaching seminar. I need you on the job. We've got all kinds of crap coming down right now and I need all hands on deck."

"No worries, Sam." Troy answered, "What's going on anyway?"

"I'm not crazy about going into it all on the phone, but let me give you the short version." Sam said, "I don't know if you ever knew Mark Simmons from Denver. We fired the son of gun last year and he's gone to the feds with some whistle-blower thing. Not much to it as far as I can tell but we're going to have to get our ducks in a row in a hurry."

"What do you need me to do?" Troy asked.

"I need you to get with your people and have them send in their laptops, iPads and even their cell phones to regional office. I'm sending an IT professional out to each regional office to gather all our documents in one place so that the attorneys can help us with due diligence. We need to be very careful, here. I don't want to hear that any of our people deleted any documents. If there is ugliness out there we need to know it. What we can't afford is anyone trying to cover their tracks by destroying evidence. That would be criminal. Do you understand?' Sam asked.

"Yes." Troy said, "I'll get on top of it right away."

"You better." Sam said, "Everyone else has a four-hour head start on you. Word might be getting around to your people. I don't trust some of your guys after the whole expense violation fiasco. I think we might be vulnerable down there."

"Maybe I should call an immediate conference call and get everyone up to snuff." Troy said.

"That's the *last* thing you should do." Sam said loudly, "Keep calm but get your people on board. Make this seem routine as can be. Don't even say the words 'whistle blower'. Tell them that due to some legal action we must collect all the electronic data we have on all our devices. They will need to FedEx their phones, iPads, and laptops to regional office to arrive on Friday. They will get them back on Monday morning."

"Do we expect media coverage on this?" Troy asked

"Probably, but not right away." Sam answered, "We should have a few days to get on top of it before the word gets out."

"If someone asks me outright about whether it is a federal investigation, can I be honest with them?" Troy asked

"I think you can say the truth; that you simply don't know all the details and don't see any reason to speculate." Sam said, "Tell them if you learn any new information, you'll keep them in the loop"

"Okay." Troy said, "I'll start right away. Anything else?"

"No, call me tomorrow and let me know how things are progressing." Sam answered.

Troy pulled out the sales roster and started with the sales representatives outside of the Atlanta area since timely shipping of the equipment could be an issue. He thought through what he would say, writing down key phrases as well as the regional office address and FedEx billing code.

It was 9:30pm when Troy finished his calls and he still had the Atlanta representatives to contact. Troy had finally completed all calls by 10pm. He felt fortunate to have been able to get in touch with everyone except Sammy Sherrill. Troy left urgent messages for him to call first thing in the morning.

Troy's stomach was growling from hunger when he went up to his hotel room to order room service. Troy called in an order for a club sandwich, fries and two light beers realizing that room service would close at 10:30.

Troy quickly jumped in the shower and afterward put on sweatpants and t-shirt in time for his generic dinner to arrive.

Troy was too tired for small talk with the room service waiter but gave the young man an additional tip to the already added in gratuity. Troy opened one of the bottles of beer and took a drink of the cold liquid, surprised at how much he valued its taste.

Troy's phone vibrated over on the nightstand. He wondered who could be calling this late and hoped that it wasn't Sammy Sherrill; Troy simply didn't have the energy. The speed dial readout displayed, "Heather".

Troy got a sick feeling in his stomach suddenly realizing that there were text messages from her that he never answered. In fact, Troy hadn't communicated with his wife since the previous evening before dinner.

He immediately picked up the phone. "Babe, I'm so sorry." Troy said into the phone. "I got tied up and I completely forgot to call."

Heather sounded distressed. "I texted you what was going on and you didn't even call. Is that job of yours all you care about?"

"No, baby." Troy said, "I haven't even seen your texts. What's going on?"

"You didn't even take time to read my texts?" Heather shouted, "Are you so busy you can't even read a two-line text from your wife? My mom is lying here in the hospital and you don't even read my texts?

"Your mom is in the hospital?" Troy asked, "What happened? Is she okay?"

"No, she's not okay." Heather said, "She might have had a stroke"

"Oh, I'm so sorry." Troy said, "Should I come home?"

"Do you even have to ask?" Heather responded, "I can't believe you would even ask me that."

"No, you're right." Troy answered, "Of course I'll come home."

Heather said. "Mom is at University Hospital. I've been here since I brought her in this morning."

"I'll be on first plane tomorrow morning." Troy said, "I'm staying out by the airport so I'm sure I can get there by noon. I'll text you my travel details."

"Okay" Heather said without emotion. There was an uncomfortable silence between them as they both considered their words and actions.

"Really Heather, I'm so sorry." Troy said sincerely, "There's no excuse for me not reading your texts."

The line remained silent.

"Ok." Troy said, "See you tomorrow. I love you."

"Me too." Heather answered, "Bye."

As soon as Troy hung up he felt guilty. In fact, he felt double guilt. He felt that he was letting Heather down by his need to work and letting Sam down by going back to Cleveland in the middle of a crisis.

Troy checked flight schedules and purchased a ticket on United that would leave Atlanta around 9am which would still give him time update Carol. He would call Sammy from the gate and give him direction regarding his equipment. Maybe with a little luck everything would come out okay.

Even though Troy was exhausted, he couldn't sleep. Knowing he had much to do before his flight kept him awake and anxious. It seemed like no time at all until morning came and it was time to take the shuttle over to the airport.

Troy called Carol at 7:30 after getting through security.

"Troy?" Carol asked, picking up the phone on the first ring. "What's going on? I heard from one of the other regional coordinators that we're under investigation by the feds." Troy thought quietly, "So much for keeping a lid on things."

"Carol, the truth is I don't know all the details." Troy said, "All I really know is that I had to call everyone on the team last night and tell them to FedEx their computers, iPads and phones to regional office to arrive tomorrow morning. I caught up with everyone but Sammy. I'll try him as soon as I hang up. If I don't catch him, I'll need you to follow up while I'm traveling to Cleveland."

"Cleveland?" Carol said shocked, "But I was counting on you to be in regional office today and tomorrow. We have lots to catch up on."

"I know." Troy said dejectedly, "Heather's mom had a stroke yesterday and I've got to go home. That is, if I still want to be married."

"That's terrible about your mother-in-law." Carol said, "Is she going to be okay?"

"I really have no idea." Troy said, "It wasn't exactly a cordial conversation last night."

"Okay." Carol said, "Go home and do what you need to do. I'll take care of things back here. If you get the chance to call sometime this afternoon that would be good."

"I will, I promise." Troy said. "Oh, and Carol...thank you. I really don't know what I would do without you right now. You are amazing."

"Thanks, Troy." Carol said sweetly. "That means a lot to me. Good luck with your trip home."

Troy immediately called Sammy. Once again, Troy got the voicemail introduction. "This is Sammy, your all-star rep from Mareno Bio; you know what to do at the beep...so do it."

The voicemail introduction represented everything about Sammy that Troy was beginning to loathe; arrogance, disrespect and irreverence. Troy left a message. "Sammy, this is Troy. I'm getting ready to board a plane but there is an urgent request that must be handled this morning before noon. Can you please call Carol in regional office as soon as you pick up this message so that she might be able to provide instructions to you? It is critically urgent for you to get this important information this morning."

Troy had a sick feeling in his stomach thinking about Sammy.

The gate agent made the boarding announcement and Troy got in line for zone five. He thought how much he looked forward to getting enough frequent flyer status with this airline to be able to board in zones one or two instead of having to fight for overhead storage for his single carry-on bag. By the time Troy got on the completely full flight he was not at all surprised to be met at the plane by a flight attendant who was sad to inform him that he would have to check his bag.

When Troy arrived in Cleveland he drove straight to University Hospital imagining his mother-in-law lying the in some vegetative state. As soon as he got to the hospital he was directed not to an intensive care unit but rather a regular inpatient unit.

Troy went to the fourth floor of the hospital looking for room 465. He walked in and found Heather sitting in a chair next to her mother's bedside. Her mom was sitting upright in the bed quietly talking to her. No apparent paralysis. No noticeable slurring of speech. In fact, Troy's mother-in-law looked fine.

"How are you doing?" Troy asked.

"Much better Troy" his mother-in-law answered, "They thought it was a stroke, but it really was only something called a TIA. I should be out of here later today or first thing tomorrow."

Troy knew that he should be relieved but couldn't shake the feeling that he had come home for nothing; that maybe he should have stayed in Atlanta. He knew this feeling was a selfish one and immediately felt guilty for entertaining it.

"I'm really glad you're here" Heather said with relief in her voice.

"Yeah, me too." Troy said. Troy sat and made small talk with his wife and mother-in-law while intermittently thinking about the latest crisis back in Atlanta.

In a few minutes Troy and Heather went out in the hall.

"Thank you for coming home." Heather said, "Yesterday was really scary to me. Mom called and said she was numb on one side of her face and that her leg wouldn't work. I took her to the ER and they took her in immediately to start running tests. Mom was weird in the way she was talking, and I was terrified. I was afraid she would end up paralyzed. They kept her last night and when the doctor came in this morning he told us that she had a TIA. I guess that is like a mini-stroke. The doctor said she'd be fine but would have to be careful since TIA's often precede a full-blown stroke. Anyway, it seemed worse than it turned out. I'm sorry you had to make the trip up here."

"Nonsense." Troy said, "You needed me, and I want to always be here for you. I know I get my priorities mixed sometimes, but you will always be first in my life."

Troy was feeling better about the trip to Cleveland. After a while Troy excused himself and slipped out into the waiting room to make a phone call.

"Hi Troy" Carol said as she answered the phone, obviously reading the display on her phone. "Is everything okay up there in Cleveland?"

"Yeah, everything is fine" Troy said, "I'll tell you about it when I get back to the office on Monday. Has Sammy contacted you yet?"

"No, but I checked my email and have a message from him." Carol said, "It seems that he has gone off on a Caribbean cruise and will be gone until next Thursday."

"Don't people request vacation around here?" Troy said, irritated.

"More like inform." Carol said, "People think it would be demeaning to have to ask for time off that they have already earned."

"Whatever." Troy said with disgust, "How do we get Sammy's equipment?"

"We don't." Carol said, "We'll send it in when he returns."

"I hate that." Troy said.

"Actually, you did very well getting everything back. Some regions had several reps that were gone on vacation." Carol said.

Well, that is some consolation, anyway." Troy said. "Anything else happening?"

"Yes." Carol said, "They put performance calibration on the calendar for three weeks from Monday."

"What is performance calibration?" Troy asked.

"That's where you get together with Sam, Greta and the other regional managers to force-rank your people and determine their performance ratings."

"Are you kidding me?" Troy said loudly, "I haven't even worked with everyone yet. How am I supposed to force-rank people?"

"Well first you've already been in the field or at least met with 7 of the team members. With your new hire for north Georgia, you only have Pam and Cassie remaining. I have you in the field with them over the next two weeks. And then you will definitely want to talk to Cheryl Masters." Carol offered.

"Cheryl, the regional manager in the northeast?" Troy asked.

"The one and only." Carol said, "She offered to help you prepare for calibration two weeks from tomorrow. But you will have to go up to Boston to meet with her."

"That's fine; I'll stay up there over that weekend before calibration." Troy said, already thinking that such a decision might trigger another disagreement with Heather.

"Okay." Carol said, "I'll make the travel arrangements. Now, put Mareno on hold and be there for Heather."

Troy said. "Thanks Carol."

Troy grabbed a cup of watered-down coffee from a vending machine and started walking back to room 465. He was almost to the doorway when his cell phone started vibrating in his pocket. It was Sam.

Troy pushed the green button to answer the phone.

"Hi Sam." Troy said.

"How's Heather's mom?" Sam asked. Troy was impressed that Sam even knew what was going on.

"She's going to be fine, actually." Troy answered, "It turned out to be a TIA rather than a stroke. It was a bit of a false alarm."

"It happens." Sam said calmly. "Women don't understand the intensity men like us have on the job. My first wife was constantly calling me with so-called emergencies. I had to learn some tricks to figure out when it was real and when she was just lonely. You'll figure it out. My second wife was a little bit better, but I think it's in their DNA. Even Janay cries wolf every now and then."

Troy couldn't believe what he was hearing. It sounded like something a man would say in the 1950s. It made Troy cringe. "I don't even know what to say." Troy said, realizing for the first time Sam's misogynist attitude towards women.

"Don't say anything." Sam answered, "You're already there now. You might as well act like you're in the moment."

"Okay." Troy said. He couldn't believe Sam's attitude about the situation. It was so outdated that Troy was dumbfounded.

"I understand you did a great job getting the word out about the data collection exercise." Sam observed. "Everybody is cooperating except that character, Sammy Sherrill."

"Yeah, he's on vacation." Troy said.

"Whatever." Sam said, "Do we really need that guy? He seems like he's always got an issue."

"I had heard that he was someone that you really liked."

Troy said quietly.

"I don't know who told you that." Sam said defensively, then immediately backtracked. "Well, whoever told you was probably right. I did hire the son of a gun. Lately, he's seems more trouble than he's worth. He still puts up pretty good sales numbers, but I want you to know if you start finding stuff you don't like you'd have my support to do whatever is necessary."

"Okay." Troy answered, "I'm not sure what I've got right now with all of the people."

"Well, you better figure it out pretty quickly." Sam said, "We have calibration coming up in a couple of weeks and I need you to have your act together."

"I know." Troy said, "I'm going to work with Cheryl Masters."

"Troy, I know." Sam said, "I asked Cheryl to set that up."

"Oh, right." Troy said, "I didn't know."

"I'm watching out for you, my friend." Sam said, "Hang in there; you're going to do fine. Sam hung up without even saying goodbye. Troy only hoped that he could continue to meet Sam's expectations.

Troy thought about Sam's sarcastic advice regarding "being in the moment" and relaxed considerably before re-entering his mother-in-law's hospital room.

Troy looked lovingly at Heather and said, "You've been here since yesterday. Why don't we go out and have a bite of dinner together and stop back by here on our way home."

Heather agreed upon her mother's urging. Troy found a nice Italian restaurant near the University called Luigi's; not too original of a name but the food and atmosphere were delightful.

Despite the fragility of conversation over the past two days, Troy and Heather were warm and loving now that they were once again face to face.

"I'm sorry for my insensitivity about your mom." Troy said.

"And I'm sorry about losing it. "Heather said, "I'm sure I sounded pitiful. I'm glad you're home. I miss you so much. I've been sleeping on your side of the bed putting my head on your pillow to feel closer to you."

"Heather, if I ever start acting like a jerk," Troy said thinking about Sam's comments about women, "Please hit me over the head or something."

Heather smiled broadly, "Be careful what you ask for." she said.

Heather's mom got out of the hospital early the next morning and the rest of the weekend seemed relaxed.

It was no time at all until Troy was on a plane headed to Jacksonville on Sunday afternoon to meet with Pam and then down to Orlando for a field day with Cassie. After completing his rounds with these last team members, Troy was ready for his visit to the northeast office to meet Cheryl Masterson, the regional manager.

Troy took an Uber ride from the hotel to northeast regional office. At 9am, he arrived at Cheryl's office. Cheryl's regional coordinator was on vacation and Cheryl greeted Troy when he arrived and buzzed him into the office. Cheryl was probably in her late fifties, maybe early sixties. She had medium length brown hair with a few streaks of gray. She wore pearl glasses and a burgundy pantsuit; a style of which

Troy hadn't seen for nearly twenty years.

"Nice to finally meet you in person." Cheryl said, "I was overseas during the national sales meeting; one of Sam's little drive by shootings"

"Where did you go?" Troy asked.

"France. Sam wanted me to fill in for him and look at a potential new product." Cheryl said, "Turned out to be a bust. Anyway, everyone has had nice things to say about you."

"Likewise." Troy said, returning the compliment.

"How are you settling into this new job?" Cheryl asked without emotion, "It's one son of a bitch, isn't it?"

Troy laughed. "Yes, that's a good way to say it."

"And you haven't even really settled down to get to know your team and you're expected to be able to properly calibrate their performance." Cheryl said with a slight smile. "What the Hell is wrong with these people?"

Once again Troy laughed, fully appreciating the way Cheryl was calling out the obvious.

"Well, no one expects you to be a damn clairvoyant or anything." Cheryl said, "But you know more than you realize about your people. You'll be surprised how accurate your impressions can be."

"That sounds encouraging." Troy said, "Where do we start?"

"We start in the break room." Cheryl said with a laugh, "I bought some Dunkin Donuts and coffee this morning and we are damn well going to enjoy them."

Troy and Cheryl spent a few minutes getting coffee and donuts before returning to Cheryl's conference room. Cheryl took a large sip of coffee as she pulled out a blue marker and drew two perpendicular lines on the white board.

"Have you spoken to Greta about the competency profiles yet?" Cheryl asked.

"Yes." Troy said, "The profiles look pretty reasonable to me."

"You're familiar then with the four major categories of the competencies?" Cheryl asked.

"Yes. They are Territory Management, Relationship Management, Product/Market Knowledge and Selling Skills/Persuasion." Troy responded.

"Exactly." Cheryl said as she wrote the four categories in the four boxes on the white board.

Cheryl handed Troy a stack of index cards.

"What are these for?" Troy asked with a smile.

"You are a go-getter, Troy." Cheryl said with a smile, "We'll get to that in a minute. Now, let me ask you about the last couple of reps you worked with."

"Okay." Troy said.

"I worked with Cassie Clair down in Orlando." Troy answered.

"Let me ask you on a scale from 1 to 10, 1 being really bad and 10 being the best you've ever seen, how was Cassie with Territory Management?" Cheryl asked.

"She was great." Troy said, "We saw ten doctors and she knew exactly what was happening with each one. I'd say she was maybe like an 8 or 9."

"And on the same scale, how was she on Product Knowledge?" Cheryl asked.

"Once again, really strong." Troy answered, "I'd say an eight."

"Relationship management?" Cheryl asked.

"Maybe a tad less, perhaps a seven." Troy said.

"Okay and what about Selling Skills?" Cheryl asked.

"She gave really good presentations although I'd love to see a bit more dialogue during her presentations." Troy observed, "I think I'd give her a seven."

"Great." Cheryl said, "Let's move on. Let's take one of your other reps. What about Yolanda?"

"Well, she's pretty new." Troy said.

"How would you rate her on Territory Management?" Cheryl asked.

"She has some work to do there." Troy said, "She's probably a five."

"Product Knowledge?" Cheryl asked.

"Actually, she was surprisingly strong." Troy said, "I think she's a seven on that."

"Relationship management?" Cheryl asked,

"Solid. Probably a six" Troy said.

"Selling Skills?" Cheryl asked.

"I'd say a five at this point." Troy answered.

"Okay." Cheryl said, "Guess what the cards are for?"

"I'm guessing you want me to rate the four categories with each of my reps?" Troy asked.

"Yes." Cheryl said, "And I want you to put the same amount of time and thought into the exercise that you did for Cassie and Yolanda. For each rep put their name on the card and then a score for Territory Management, Product Knowledge, Relationship Management and Selling Skills. Please don't over think this. I'm going to go check my email. I'll be back in five minutes."

Troy quickly did his assignment, flipping one index card at a time and filling it out for the four categories of competencies. In a matter of minutes Troy had completed cards for his entire team.

Cheryl was back in about ten minutes with another plate of donuts and a fresh cup of coffee.

"Are you finished?" Cheryl asked.

"Yes." Troy said, "But I hope I'm not making gut judgments or being unfair."

"You are definitely making gut judgments." Cheryl said, "Get used to it. Besides, over time you will gain better and better perspective. But don't discount your early observations. And remember no one is holding you to these numeric scores. They serve as an initial indicator to help you identify who in your team is top, middle and bottom in overall competencies... And by the way, I've done this repeatedly. It is amazing how remarkably accurate these so-called gut judgments actually are."

Cheryl went to the white board and drew a table with several columns and about twenty rows.

"Okay." Cheryl said, "Let's put your scores on the whiteboard."

Name	TM	PK	RM	SS	Overall		Tenure
Yolanda	5	7	6	5	23		New
Cassie	8	8	7	7	30		3
Lester	7	6	5	5	23		4
Pam	6	6	6	6	24		3
Rodney	7	7	8	6	28		4
Cindy	8	6	6	5	25		7
Sammy	8	7	8	7	30		8
Danny	6	6	6	5	23		5
Terri	8	7	7	7	29		6
Rachael	5	5	5	5	20		New

"Looking at your scores, what do you see?" Cheryl asked.

"Well, Sammy, Cassie and Terri are the best I've got." Troy said almost painfully as he thought about how difficult it is to work with Sammy.

"What else?" Cheryl asked.

"Danny, Yolanda, Lester and Rachael are all at the bottom." Troy said, "I guess I would expect that of the new people like Yolanda and Rachael, but Danny and Lester have tenure and should be much better at skills."

"You also have two vacancies right now." Cheryl said, "What is the minimum score you would be hoping for in each category for a new employee?"

"I'd be looking for no less than 7 across the board, a 28 overall." Troy said confidently.

"Interesting." Cheryl noted, "Then, you wouldn't hire most of the folks on your current team."

The realization hit Troy hard. "Wow." He said, "That's

really disturbing."

"Well, it means you have some work to do." Cheryl said, "You will either need to coach your team up or you may have to coach some of them out."

"That's a little overwhelming to think about right now." Troy admitted.

"Well, sooner or later you'll be able to make the call." Cheryl said, "But for now, let's go back to the table on the white board. Notice I left a couple of blank columns."

"I noticed that." Troy said.

"Now that we've looked at competencies I want to next look at sales results." Cheryl said in a matter of fact manner."

"Should we look at volume or growth?" Troy asked.

"Yes." Cheryl answered with a chuckle.

"I'm not sure which to weight more." Troy said.

"Well, why don't you weigh them equally? I like to `think of it this way. High volume and high growth are the top tier. Low volume and low growth are the bottom tier. Everyone else is in the middle." Cheryl suggested.

"That makes sense." Troy said. He had his sales results table on his iPad as he stepped up to the white board and filled in the open column.

"The final thing I want to look at is how coachable the rep is." Cheryl suggested, "You can use your initial impressions here and label everyone high, medium and low in their desire and ability to be coached."

Troy filled in the last column of the table.

"I want to put this spreadsheet on my computer." Troy said, "And I think I'll color code it, so it will make more sense."

"You're a damned superstar, Troy." Cheryl said," I was

going to suggest the same thing."

Troy' final worksheet was as follows:

Name	TM	PK	RM	SS	Overall	Results	Coachable
Yolanda	5	7	6	5	23	LL	H
Cassie	8	8	7	7	30	HH	M
Lester	7	6	5	5	23	LL	M
Pam	6	6	6	6	24	LM	M
Rodney	7	7	8	6	28	LM	M
Cindy	8	6	6	5	25	HL	M
Sammy	8	7	8	7	30	HH	L
Danny	6	6	6	5	23	LL	L
Terri	8	7	7	7	29	HM	H
Rachael	5	5	5	5	20	LH	H

"What has this little exercise taught you thus far?" Cheryl asked with a chuckle.

"Lots of things, actually." Troy said, "Some of which surprises me a bit."

"Like?' Cheryl asked.

"Like the fact that Sammy Sherrill is a pain to deal with but is probably my best overall rep. And that Cassie is also one of my best and I haven't paid much attention to her because she is quiet and unassuming" Troy observed. "And then there's Danny and Lester that should be doing much, much better considering their tenure."

"What do you see with Terri?" Cheryl asked.

"Someone with great potential that needs some help to be absolutely great." Troy said.

"Wow." Cheryl said, "Those are some pretty powerful observations from someone who said this morning that he didn't know how to evaluate people."

"Interesting." Troy acknowledged, now feeling more confident in his own judgment. "I think there is even more here to learn."

"Go on." Cheryl said.

"This can almost serve as a coaching guide to combine with some of the things I learned a few weeks ago at the coaching seminar. One of the key elements of that class was making sure that we coach the right WHAT." Troy observed. "Looking at the four categories of competencies provides a clue as to where to start. For example, Cindy is great with territory management but needs help in selling skills. Looking at things this way should help me prepare for work sessions."

"Well, work session planning is a whole different topic but you're right, this is one element." Cheryl reinforced. "Maybe after calibration we can get together again to discuss how to prepare for work sessions to get the most of each one."

"I'd like that, Cheryl." Troy said.

"Does this exercise help you to prioritize your time, at all?" Cheryl asked.

"Maybe." Troy said, "But aren't I supposed to give equal coaching time to all of my team members?"

"If you only had 5 or 6 direct reports like you would in some companies, I would agree." Cheryl said, "But when you get your vacancies filled you will have twelve. Some are going to need more attention than others."

"I guess I can see that." Troy acknowledged.

"Like, let's take Sammy Sherrill as an example." Cheryl said, "How often do you need to work with Sammy as opposed to maybe Terri or Yolanda?"

"Well, Sammy and Terri's territories are extremely important to the region because of size and growth, but Terri is far more coachable. Terri wants me to work with her where Sammy sees little value in what I bring to the work session. I guess that until I earn Sammy's trust and respect, I would probably get a bigger bang for my buck working with Terri."

"And Yolanda?" Cheryl asked.

"Well, she's a sponge and she will grow on every work session, but she also has a low volume, low growth territory. Even if she makes major gains in skills it will take a while for that to translate into a real contribution to the team in sales results." Troy observed.

"Obviously you will work with everyone on the team but some you need to invest more time with to gain quick business results." Cheryl said, "If you had to pick the top three people to work with, who would they be?"

"I already mentioned Terri. She's important because she has volume, growth, coachability and good competencies. I also would pick Cindy because some of her skills are strong but selling skills are weak and she has high volume but low growth. I think with good coaching we could quickly turn a low growth territory into high growth. This would make a difference to team performance."

"I like the way you think." Cheryl said, "Who would you pick next?"

"Probably Cassy because she has a high-volume territory

and is coachable and has specific skill deficits that I could help improve." Troy said.

"There's a lot to think about, for sure." Cheryl said, "The thing is you can be very effective if you routinely look at your time like this and ask yourself the kind of questions we are asking right now."

"Yes, I can see that." Troy acknowledged.

"One more question." Cheryl said, "What about new hires? How much time should you devote to them?"

"Well, they need a lot of hand-holding." Troy said thinking out loud, "But I could delegate a lot to other team members."

"Can I offer another perspective?' Cheryl asked.

"Sure." Troy said.

"Think about each time you've started a new job over the years." Cheryl said, "When were you most open to feedback and guidance?"

"The first few weeks." Troy said with a smile.

"Yes." Cheryl said, "Some of the feedback and suggestions I'm making right now would seem like interference to you in a few months. It's human nature. We are excited to learn at the beginning and we also bond to whoever teaches us during that period."

"That's true." Troy acknowledged, "The very first guy I got to train back at Forbes is now my best friend."

"And it can be a wonderful thing to delegate." Cheryl said, "But if I was your boss I would have rather had your friend bonding to me...and doing things the way I want to see them done."

"I guess I can see that." Troy said, "But isn't there a chance to bond the new person to the team through delegation?"

"I'm not suggesting that you never delegate." Cheryl clarified, "But remember that your own personal influence on an employee will never be greater than the first few weeks on the job. It is a golden opportunity that many managers fail to take advantage of."

"That's good advice, Cheryl." Troy acknowledged, "Thank you."

"Now, let's shift gears." Cheryl said, "In preparation for the calibration session Monday, what documentation will you bring with you?"

"That's the thing." Troy said, "Brian completed a year-end review on each team member but there are absolutely no field reports from work sessions. And the year-end reviews don't exactly match up with sales performance."

"You mean the performance ratings are inconsistent?" Cheryl asked.

"Yes." Troy said, "Like Danny was given an exceptional rating even though the table we put together shows him lacking performance no matter how one would rate it. And Pam Smith was rated needs improvement even though her performance is in the middle of the pack."

"What about other documentation?' Cheryl asked, "Resource utilization reports, call reports, weekly reports, those kinds of things?"

"Very spotty." Troy said, "I don't know what to bring to show how each person is performing except for sales results. I get the feeling that Brian may have rated people on how well he liked them. I don't want to throw him under the bus but there is little documentation to support his ratings."

"I agree that there is little reason to vilify Brian." Cheryl acknowledged, "My guess is that Sam and Greta are already aware that there were pretty significant gaps. My advice would be to bring the work we've done today, acknowledge that there are gaps in documentation and that your assessments are very early in the process. Don't try to oversell your opinions and instead ask for the input of the calibration team. And listen but do so with a discerning ear. Sometimes, opinions are thrown out without anything more than an impression. You need to know these perceptions but don't consider them as gospel."

"That sounds like good advice." Troy said, "I don't want to look incompetent."

"At your tenure as a manager, the only way you can look incompetent is if you try to appear more confident and self-assured than you really are." Cheryl offered. "I'll be there, too. I'll back you up on what we've done today. One other thing though. Make sure you describe the steps you will take to provide accurate documentation moving forward."

"Yes." Troy said, "That makes sense."

"Remember, this process we went through today will get better and more accurate as you gain more exposure to your team. Your observations and documentation will make next year's calibration session much easier for you. You will be far more confident as you gain a continuum of observations." Cheryl added.

"Is there anything else you would suggest I do?" Troy asked.

"Yes." Cheryl said, "In time, let your people do a self

assessment and one of you, as well. They won't always be on target but even that will tell you something. People who are self-aware are usually coachable. It can open whole new avenue for change. You'll also learn more about how your people view you and how you might serve them better."

"I know that's true." Troy said, "What you've shared with me today gives me a good start for sure. Thank you."

Cheryl changed the subject.

"What are you doing over the weekend?" Cheryl asked.

"I'm not sure." Troy said, "I'll be alone. Maybe enjoy the changing seasons. Autumn is really beautiful up here."

"Enjoy it Troy." Cheryl said, "I'll see you at calibration on Monday. Have a great weekend."

"Thank you for all of your help, Cheryl." Troy said with great sincerity. "I learned much from you."

"Yeah, yeah." Cheryl said with a smile, "Always good to placate us old folks."

Then Cheryl did something that seemed out of character. She put her arms around Troy and gave him a hug.

"You're a good man, Troy." Cheryl said, "I'm glad to have you as a colleague."

Troy went back to the hotel and decided to change clothes before going down to the lounge for a drink. He turned on the television and caught the following news story:

> "Today, the federal government announced that a local Boston company, Mareno Biosciences is the target of an investigation brought about by a former employee who claims that Mareno unduly and unlawfully influenced physicians and hospital administrators to

use their product. Within these charges are claims that Mareno made direct payments to physicians amounting to thousands of dollars in exchange for their support or influence in hospital buying decisions. There are also charges that Mareno Biosciences employees were present for patient procedures and may have even assisted physicians during these procedures. A spokesperson for Mareno claims that the company has always maintained the highest standards to ensure compliance with all laws and regulations and is fully cooperating with the federal investigation."

Troy's stomach felt sick as he heard this breaking news story knowing that things could get very challenging over the next few weeks.

QUESTIONS TO CONSIDER:

1) Is Sammy Sherrill an asset or liability to Mareno and Troy's team?

2) When there is a conflict between work and personal crisis, how do you decide which is more important?

3) Do the quick rating exercise for your team.
    a. Were there any surprises?
    b. Did you gain any of the same learnings that Troy had?
    c. Is there anything you will do differently?

4) Do you agree with Troy's choices on priority sales representatives? Why?

CHAPTER TWELVE: STAR WORK SESSIONS

"I can't believe we are finally getting to move into our house!" Heather said with excitement. "It seems like forever since the President's Cup trip. I am excited to sign all the papers tomorrow."

The closing was scheduled for 9am the next morning. Heather and Troy would be able to have access to their new home right after they signed all the papers. The closing while exciting to Heather was somewhat stressful for Troy. Although he loved the new house the financial commitment seemed astronomical.

Due to Troy and Heather's high credit scores and Troy's significant bump in pay, the couple qualified for a mortgage payment nearly twice what they were paying in rent back in Cleveland.

Troy knew that the price of the house was only the beginning. Moving from a three-bedroom ranch to a five-bedroom, four-bath custom built home meant that they would need to buy furniture for all those additional rooms. New furniture meant new accessories. Then, of course, was the maintenance of the lawn and the pool. Troy hoped that Heather would soon start working full-time at her new job to help contribute.

The closing took less than thirty minutes, a general flurry of documents signed and dated by both Troy and Heather. When the last document was signed the realtor, Kiki Clossen stood up, smiled and handed Troy the keys. Troy smiled but couldn't help but think he was signing his life away.

Heather hugged Kiki as if she were some close female relative. Troy inwardly smiled knowing that Kiki would happily deposit her commission check and never be heard from again.

"I love you so much." Heather said, "In my wildest fantasies I never thought I'd someday be living in a beautiful home like this. Thank you, Troy,"

"Well, you've contributed to this as well." Troy said in a charming manner.

"Thanks for saying that, Baby." Heather said, "I don't make as much as you do but I appreciate your recognizing my part in this."

"You've forgotten those early days when you were paying all the bills." Troy said, "At different times we have had different roles in the finances. The thing is we've earned this together."

The couple drove to the new house impressed with their new neighborhood in the gated community. They would no longer have to stop at the guard house to register now that Kiki had turned over the gate sensors that opened the gates as they approached.

"I feel like royalty." Heather said "Look at this neighborhood. Wait until Mom and Dad come down to visit."

The community was in a wooded area of Alpharetta. Each lawn was meticulously groomed by a lawn service. No one in this neighborhood would be caught mowing their own lawn. Every house had trees and flowered bushes. The driveways were constructed with pavers rather than poured cement or asphalt. Some of the houses had special garage doors for golf carts, one of the accepted modes of transportation within the community.

Troy kept thinking of Sam's reaction to pictures of the property he had shown during the national meeting.

Sam laughed broadly and said, "Well, Son. Nothing makes for a harder working regional manager than a huge mortgage...unless of course, it would be a new baby, too."

Troy hoped that the baby thing wouldn't happen for many years.

When they pulled up to their new house Troy looked over at Heather and she had tears in her eyes.

"That beautiful house is my home." She said with a sniffle.

Troy and Heather got out of the car and walked up to the front door. Troy unlocked the deadbolt and opened the door. Then he looked at Heather lovingly and picked her up in his arms, carrying her across their new threshold.

Troy's cell phone began vibrating in his pocket. The number was a Boston 617 area code and although Troy didn't recognize it he thought it must be someone at Mareno. Troy placed Heather back to the floor.

"Good morning, this is Troy." Troy said as he answered.

"Hi Troy. This is Patrick O'Malley, chief counsel for Mareno" said the voice at the other end of the conversation.

"Hi Patrick." Troy answered, "What can I do for you?"

"We've completed the first round of searches on your team's electronic communications for the investigation." Patrick said. "Things look pretty good for the most part. I do have a few concerns, though."

"Okay." Troy said, "What can I do to help?"

"I think we will want to visit with a few of your reps, specifically Danny Bowman, Cindy Sherman and Sammy Sherrill." Patrick said.

"Can I ask what your concerns are?" Troy asked.

"For a couple of them, it's probably no more than getting clarification on some of their email communication but for one there were several things deleted the day that we asked for the machines. That's the one that concerns me the most. Anyway, I can't share any details because you too, have some potential liability." Patrick said.

Troy's heart dropped to his stomach as if he were on the first downward slope of a roller coaster.

"Me?" Troy asked, "Why would I have liability?"

"Long story." Patrick said, "I don't think you should be worried. Still, when we come down to Atlanta we will want to have an interview with you, too. Can we get the four of you in regional office on Friday?"

"You mean like the day after tomorrow?" Troy asked almost in shock.

"Yes." Patrick said, "I will be coming down tomorrow and will bring Frank Delaney along with me. You remember Frank, our compliance attorney?"

"Sure, okay." Troy said, "I'll call Carol and set up a schedule."

"That's sounds good. Make it 90 minutes for each interview." Patrick said, "And by the way, we will want to talk to Carol too. I'd prefer that you don't share many details with her right now."

"Okay." Troy said. "Do you want to get together tomorrow night for dinner?"

"That probably wouldn't be a good idea until our official interview is over." Patrick answered. "I'll be at your office at 8am on Friday. Let's save your interview for last."

As Troy ended the call he tried in a panic to think of anything that he could have done that would have put himself or Mareno Biosciences at risk. While he was fairly in tune with industry compliance rules, he wondered if he could have somehow stepped over some boundary without knowing it. He must have looked anxious as Heather came around the corner and looked at Troy with concern.

"Is everything okay?" Heather asked.

"I think so." Troy answered, "It was the company attorney. About the investigation. I'm sure everything is fine. I do have to be at the office on Friday now. The movers are supposed to be here tomorrow and the worst of things with the move should be done before I have to go to work."

"You're going to leave me to deal with all of the unpacking?" Heather asked showing some irritation.

"Baby, I can't help it." Troy said, "Besides we will have all weekend."

Heather shook her head and walked upstairs. Troy felt as though the pressure was crushing him.

"She has no idea what I'm going through." Troy whispered to himself. Then, letting out his breath he thought, "And that's probably a good thing."

When Troy and Heather returned to the hotel one last time before moving in to the new house, Troy was glad to hear Heather say that she wanted to go shopping for some home accessories. This would give him some time to think through all he would need to do over the next few days, as well as contacting Carol to get her help in setting up Friday's meetings. He gladly handed Heather the car keys and told her to take her time and enjoy herself.

Troy called Carol and found her to be calm as always. "This is pretty standard stuff." Carol said. "If we only have a few that they want to interview at this point, this is a good thing."

"What about you and me?" Troy asked.

"It would be obvious that they would want to talk to both of us." Carol observed, "They want to make sure that there was no direction from regional office that could be misinterpreted. My advice to you is to relax. I've been through this kind of thing before and its no big deal. For someone as ethical as you are, Troy, it really is nothing."

"You are amazing, Carol." Troy said, "I am lucky to have you. Thank you."

"No problem." Carol answered, "I'll make all the arrangements and we will have our interviews ready to go for Friday. In the meantime, get some rest and help Heather with the move."

"Okay." Troy acknowledged, "I'll be in the office around 7am on Friday morning."

Troy had completed the call when his phone rang again. This time it was Dennis.

"Well, Hello my friend." Dennis said immediately when Troy picked up. "Wanted to check with you and see how things are going."

"Things are absolutely nuts." Troy said, "I had no idea this job would be this encompassing. It never lets up."

"Yeah, I know." Dennis said, "With the federal investigation it will get even crazier. How's the move coming along?"

"We closed on the new monster home." Troy said with a laugh, "Two people, five bedrooms, four baths. Heather loves it, though."

"Well, I'm sure you get a lot for your money in Atlanta." Dennis said.

"Actually, I'll be lucky if I don't choke on this mortgage." Troy said grimacing.

"I should have told you about the five-minute wow factor." Dennis said.

"What are you talking about?" Troy said.

"Oh, something I learned around our third move." Dennis replied. "I learned that when family or friends come to your new house for the first time they look around and say 'WOW'. That affect lasts about five minutes and is the only time they ever pay attention to your house. The next time they come, they take off their shoes, sit on your furniture, watch TV; whatever, but the one thing they never comment on again is your house. I called this the 'Five Minute Wow Factor' and figured I was paying one heck of a lot of money for it. I finally decided that whatever we bought we would buy entirely for us, not for the reaction of family and friends. At some point, your mother-in-law figures out that her daughter made a good decision." Dennis said with a laugh.

"I think we definitely got caught up in all of that." Troy said, "Well, for now it is keeping Heather excited and happy which is good considering how demanding work is."

"Oh yes." Dennis said, "Sounds like work has earned a pretty big slice of Life's Pie."

"Definitely." Troy acknowledged. "Even though you warned me, I still find the other slices getting smaller. I think I underestimated is how addicting this position could be. When I was selling, it was more like a job. But this job, well, this is my life. As crazy as it is and as demanding as it is, I really, truly love it."

"Don't end up having a regional manager title and nothing else." Dennis said seriously.

"Okay." Troy said, "I have to tell you I'm concerned about this investigation. I keep thinking if there is anything that I could have done wrong."

"If you have to think about it, you're going to be fine." Dennis said, "Believe me, those who will be in trouble know exactly what they've done wrong. There will be some casualties but I don't see you as one of them. The standard, of course is higher now that you are a regional manager. You will have to be much clearer in what you communicate on a day-to-day basis to make sure no one can misinterpret your direction."

"That's funny." Troy said, "That's the second time I've heard that today. Carol said something very similar."

"Yes." Dennis said, "That's one of the challenges of

leading people. I can point you to a couple of great resources for written communication that can help. There are a variety of things that can make a difference. One thing I learned was to cut out all the flowery stuff when writing and instead use bulleted facts. Still, there are many things that can help you. I'll email some information that you can use for follow up."

"Thanks." Troy said, "That would be helpful."

"How did calibration go?" Dennis asked.

"It went fine thanks to Cheryl." Troy answered, "She helped a lot. Still, they held me to a low standard this year. Next year I will have to be far more prepared with proper documentation."

"Yeah, the honeymoon period of a new job is great." Dennis acknowledged with a laugh, "But It doesn't last very long around here."

"That's the truth." Troy said, "Well, I have a couple of hours before Heather gets back. I think I need to prepare for my work sessions next week since my Friday will be tied up with the attorneys."

"Good luck with that." Dennis said.

"Thanks." Troy said, "And seriously, thanks for keeping in touch. It really means a lot to me."

"No problem." Dennis said, "Talk to you later."

Troy pulled out his computer and looked at who he had scheduled for work sessions the following week. Monday and Tuesday, he had planned to work with Lester in Tampa Bay and then Cassy over in Orlando on Wednesday and Thursday.

Troy started by looking at the calibration spreadsheet he had used the previous week.

Lester had a lower set of competencies and was working

in a low volume territory with low growth.

Troy looked at they documentation that was available and found that Lester underutilized resources such a starter kits and promotional speaker programs compared to other sales representatives. There was no call data but in the annual performance review Brian had noted that Lester often called on physicians that were not busy rather than going after those who could be considered high volume potential.

With such little documentation Troy wondered exactly what he should be doing to prepare for a work session. Then he remembered that Cheryl Masters had told him she had some solid information that could help him with work session planning.

Troy had put Cheryl on speed dial and he found her name and pressed the "call" button on his phone.

"Cheryl Master's office, Sally speaking." said the voice on the other end of the line.

"Hey Sally, this is Troy down in the southeast." Troy said, "Sorry I missed you when I was up visiting Cheryl. How was the vacation?"

"Amazing." Sally said, "We went to St. Thomas. I didn't want to come back."

"I've been there once." Troy acknowledged, "What a beautiful place."

"Yes. But now I'm back in beautiful Boston." Sally said laughing, "What can I do for you?"

"Is Cheryl in the office today?" Troy asked, "I wanted to talk to her about work session planning."

"She's on the road again working on some project for Sam" Sally answered, "You might call Scott Sedman down in the southwest. He was working on something official with Cheryl on that topic earlier in the year. I don't think anything was adopted by the company, but he would probably be good guy to call and I know he's in the office today."

"Thanks for the tip, Sally." Troy said, "I'll give him a call."

Troy had met Scott briefly during the national sales meeting and then got to know him a little bit better at the calibration session. Before Troy, Scott was the youngest of the regional managers, in his early thirties. He was sharp-witted and bright; sometimes a little too much so. Cheryl had made the comment to Troy that Scott was always "the smartest guy in the room".

Troy knew that he would have to put his own insecurities at bay to ask Scott for advice. Still, he was curious to know more about what Cheryl and Scott had concocted for work session planning.

Troy entered the number for southwest region office on the phone.

"Good afternoon. southwest region office for Mareno Biosciences. This is Dawn Matthews." The answering voice said.

"Hi Dawn." Troy said enthusiastically, "This is Troy Noble. Is Scott available?"

"Well hello Troy." Dawn said, "How are things going? I've heard many good things about you."

"Thanks Dawn." Troy said, "Things are going great. I'm looking forward to meeting you one of these days."

"That would be fun." Dawn said playfully, "I think you'd love our Dallas office, y'all."

"I hear enough y'alls down here in Atlanta." Troy said in a

teasing voice. "Besides, you sound more like a Midwesterner."

"So right you are." Dawn said, "I grew up in Ohio but now Dallas is home. Anyway, Scott is off the phone now. Let me patch you through. Have a great day."

Scott picked up the phone.

"Troy, the newbie." Scott said, "How are things going down in Atlanta?"

"Pretty crazy right now but I'm hanging in there." Troy answered.

"I heard you have Patrick and Frank visiting you tomorrow." Scott said, "That should be fun. They're coming down here next week. That Mark Simmons was a piece of work. Since Denver was in my region, I'm sure I'll be bogged down in this for a while."

"Yeah. I don't know much about the whole thing right now." Troy said, "I'm sure I'll learn more soon."

"You're probably better off not knowing much." Scott said, "I can't believe the betrayal of people like Simmons. Still, I'm sure you didn't call to talk about all of this."

"No, you're right." Troy said, "I called to ask you about the work you did with Cheryl around work session planning."

"Not that it matters but actually it was the work Cheryl did with me on what I called <u>The Ultimate Work Session.</u> It was my idea, but Cheryl helped work some of the details." Scott said.

"Is there some kind of document that outlines the topic?" Troy said.

"In progress, my friend." Scott said, "Don't you want to know how this whole thing started?"

"Sure." Troy said acting interested.

"Well one day I got to thinking about raising my son, Scott junior and I thought what would happen if I knew I only had 10-12 days in a whole year to guide and coach him. I figured that I would really take the time to plan for such special times to impart to him the things that really mattered. I thought that there is no way I would show up and hope that I could help him with something. Well, that's how I equated the time I get with each one of my sales representatives. I get no more than 10-12 days in a year to make a difference. I figured I really need to plan for these work sessions." Scott outlined.

"That's an interesting perspective, Scott." Troy said

"I thought so." Scott said, "I started asking myself what all I would need to do to really prepare for these times in the field. I came up with two things that I always needed to do."

"Okay, I'm listening." Troy said.

"I figured that on every work session I needed to help improve business performance and sales representative skill development" Scott outlined. "To do this I had to get very, very good at diagnosis. You can't coach what you can't identify."

"I get that." Troy acknowledged, "In the coaching course I took they called that coaching the right WHAT. The guy that ran the seminar had an expression that said, 'if you can name it and understand it, you can change it'

"Yeah. I think I went to the same seminar." Scott said, "Anyway, I have a whole series of things I review regarding territory level business performance."

"What do you look at?" Troy asked.

"First I compare the territory's sales results against region and company averages. I look at trends since the last work session. You know, is the territory improving, declining or staying the same compared to the last time I worked with the rep? Then, I look at how the territory is achieving the business milestones set in the business plan."

"Good idea." Troy acknowledged.

"Then I get really granular and look at specific accounts. I look to see which customers have change positively or negatively since the last work session. You'd be surprised how many times that a territory shows no growth because some accounts are growing while others are contracting. Sometimes, stopping the bleeding from the decliners can turn a territory into positive gain."

"That makes sense." Troy said.

"I then look at call numbers, expense management and resource utilization." Scott said.

"But I didn't think Mareno requires call numbers to be reported." Troy said.

"They don't, but you need to." Scott said, "Your people will complain and groan, but you have to have that kind of information."

"Good to know." Troy said, "It's part of my business plan to improve sales force effectiveness. Why expense reporting. What are you looking for?"

"Oh my gosh." Scott exclaimed, "Expense reporting tells you everything. Look at the time and date stamps on receipts. They tell you a great deal; they reveal things like when people go through tolls, what time and how often they buy gas, where they do in-service programs. This is like the mother lode of activity information."

"It seems a little big brother to me." Troy said.

"That's because you are in the trusting stage of management." Scott said with a laugh. "There are three stages; first you trust everyone, then you get screwed over and then you trust no one. Finally, you get sane and you trust but only with verification."

"That sounds cynical." Troy said wincing.

"Maybe, but you'll soon learn." Scott said.

"Anything else you're looking for regarding territory business performance?" Troy asked.

"Yes." Scott said, "I'm looking for any obvious account opportunities that need attention and patterns of purchasing that might indicate that we need a different approach. Remember, that no matter how much you plead very few sales representatives routinely analyze their business. Therefore, if you spend some time doing analysis you will always bring extra value to the work session."

"That makes sense." Troy said, "What about sales representative skill development? What do you do to prepare in that regard?"

"I'm looking for a good diagnosis there too." Scott said, "I'm looking for the four competency areas and evaluating how the rep is on all four. I look at previous field reports to see what I coached last time and whether there is any improvement. I look at email communication from the rep. I look at whether action items from the last work session were completed. I ask myself what the person does that most contribute to a successful performance. I also look for evidence of how well the person interacts with other team members."

"That's a lot to think about." Troy said, "What

documentation do you look at?"

"I already mentioned previous field reports." Scott said, "These are critical because they help make sure that I'm coaching a continuum of performance rather than hitting one issue one time and another the next. Ideally, someone should be able to look at the field reports and see exactly how they've progressed over time."

"Cheryl said the same thing." Troy observed.

"Of course." Scott said, "Where do you think she got it?"

Troy smiled.

"In addition to the field reports I look at email communication, notes I might have put in file, the previous year's annual performance review and the quick rating information that you reviewed with Cheryl." Scott continued

"It's good to know I was on the right track with some of this." Troy said.

"The important thing is to understand what you are trying to accomplish on each work session. I always outline two goals for the work session. The two goals always answer these two questions:

    1) What is the most critical business issue I need to work on to improve business performance?

    2) What is the most critical skill issue I need to work on to improve territory performance?

I always send the answers to these two questions, in other words the goals, to the sales representative and ask them to either agree or modify the objectives prior to the work session."

"That's a really good idea." Troy said, "Let me write that down."

"Let me ask you this." Scott said, "Tell me how you conduct a work session?"

"Usually, I meet the rep for breakfast or coffee no later than eight. We talk about what's going on in the territory and how the rep thinks things are going." Troy said, "Sometimes we review the agenda for the day and then we pretty much get after it.

"What about during the day?" Scott asked.

"Well, I try to recognize all the things the rep is doing well, and I acknowledge those things." Troy said.

"Anything else?" Scott asked.

"Well, eventually I will also provide coaching feedback." Troy said, "When I'm invited."

"You must have been talking to Dennis." Scott said.

"You got it." Troy said.

"He's right in theory." Scott said, "But recognize that you might not have time to wait."

"Okay." Troy said.

"All right." Scott said, "You have a good approach to work sessions but let me give you a couple of suggestions to make them better. First, when you're still in the coffee shop review the objectives of the work session. Next, when you review the agenda also discuss what role each of you will play with each customer. Sometimes, the rep will want you to support them, other times they might want you to sell and other times observe. Know your role."

"That's good advice." Troy acknowledged.

"Then get any issues or concerns on the table." Scott continued, "And if you are going to be tied up on a conference call or with some other interruption make sure you discuss this up front. There's nothing worse than having your manager mess up your day with unexpected interruptions."

"That's a really good point." Troy said, "That seems to happen quite a bit around here."

"Yes." Scott said, "And I have another rule for myself. I only accept calls from Sam and my wife, and then only if it is urgent. I figure that I need to give my best to the sales representative I'm working with and I can't do that if I'm talking on the phone. Really, the same thing applies to email and text messages."

"Hard to do." Troy said.

"Think of the message you're sending when you accept phone calls or answer texts or email." Scott said, "You're telling the rep that they are a low priority and by extension that their performance is a low priority. If that is true, then stay home. I do work sessions to help the sales rep get better and get much better results. I won't let anything get in the way."

"Got it." Troy said, "Totally understand."

"During the actual work session, what do you do before each call?" Scott probed.

"Confirm my role on the call?" Troy asked.

"Sure." Scott said, "But also discuss exactly what the sales rep is trying to accomplish on the call. This means defining where the customer is right now regarding our product and where the sales rep wants to take them on this call. This is absolutely the most important thing you can do to help the sales rep gain results. And don't accept call objectives like 'sell more product'."

"I have to work on that." Troy acknowledged.

"Well the best way to do this is for you to ask yourself what you would like to accomplish on the call." Scott said. "We get lazy answers regarding call objectives because we haven't thought through things ourselves."

"That makes sense." Troy said.

"Do you do one or two-day work sessions?" Scott asked.

"I'm beginning to do two-day sessions." Troy answered.

"What time do you finish the field time on the second day?" Scott asked.

"Whatever time the rep stops." Troy said.

"Think about that." Scott said, "If the rep wants to impress you they will work as long as possible. Yet, the feedback you provide is critical to their growth. Take command of the work session up front and tell the rep you want to stop for feedback no later than 3pm. The feedback is what will help the sales representative improve. You simply can't shortchange that."

"I can do that." Troy said.

"When do you write the field report?" Scott asked.

"Friday on my office day." Troy answered

"I can't even remember what I had for breakfast on Tuesday by the time Friday rolls around." Scott said, "How in the world will I remember with clarity everything I discussed to help a sales representative develop? When you stop at 3pm on the second day, write the document together. It will double the impact and free up your Fridays."

"That seems logical." Troy acknowledged.

"It has been a life-saver for me." Scott said.

"I've been writing everything down." Troy said, "Anything else I need to know to improve field days?"

"Follow up." Scott answered, "If you agree to actions that the sales rep is to do, write it on your calendar and make sure you follow up. This is probably the biggest difference between success and failure of creating improvement. Every manager has all these things he or she asks for, but it is a rare manager that makes sure these things are accomplished. Be the exceptional manager on this and you will see improvement in each of your people."

"Thanks Scott." Troy said, "You've really helped a lot."

"Great." Scott said, "I hate to be rude, but I've got a conference call in five minutes. Good luck with the attorneys tomorrow. I hope I've been able to help you."

Troy's head was spinning with all that Scott outlined regarding work sessions. He also recognized that he needed more than a few minutes to prepare for next week's work sessions. He hoped that while the movers were delivering furniture tomorrow that he would be able to pull the data he needed to prepare for the work sessions he would have the following week in Florida.

Troy accessed the Notes application on his iPad and wrote the following:

1) Review business plan progress
2) Pull expense reports for Cassy and Lester and review
3) Review account level performance in Cassy and Lester's territory
4) Send out work session objectives to Cassy and Lester by email
5) Prepare data portion of Field Reports in preparation for work sessions

Troy had finished making the notes when he heard The rustling of plastic shopping bags in the hallway. Heather had returned to the hotel with her new treasures. Troy went to the door and opened it so that Heather could bring the bags inside.

"I got so many bargains." Heather said excitedly, "I can't wait to show you all of my treasures!"

Heather put several large shopping bags on the bed and Troy could see some were filled with accent pillows, candles, vases and other "sit around stuff" that at this moment had nowhere to be placed.

"Oh, yeah." Heather said, "Our Visa Gold wouldn't go through at Macy's. We couldn't have reached our credit limit, could we?"

"I'll call them," Troy said, "We may have to take it easy until we adjust to the new mortgage."

Once again, Troy's stomach began to churn.

QUESTIONS TO CONSIDER:

1) How much time is optimal for you to fully analyze a direct report's business performance?

2) What documents do you review before providing feedback on skills/competencies?

3) How much time is optimal for an employee feedback session?

4) How do you ensure follow-up on agreed upon action items?

5) What is the right balance for your family between debt and comfort?

CHAPTER THIRTEEN: THE STAR TOOLBOX

Troy arrived at the office on Friday morning dreading the day of attorney interviews. Carol was entering the building when Troy also pulled up.

"You're amazing." Troy said, "Just because I came in a 7am didn't mean I expected you to."

"Oh, I wanted to make sure everything was ready." Carol said, "I brought some pastries too. We don't want the lawyers to be hungry and cranky."

Troy and Carol entered the office together. While Carol opened the box of pastries Troy started the coffee maker.

"Make it strong." Carol said, "I need extra juice to make things work well today."

"I'm going to need to prepare for work sessions next week." Troy said, "I also want to look at the territories that have been underperforming such as Lester, Danny and even Gil's old territory. I want to look for anything that might be common to these geographies. Can you pull the account level data for these territories?"

"Sure." Carol said, "First, let me get things organized for the attorneys and then I'll pull together the data you need."

Troy poured a cup of coffee as soon as it was brewed and went back to his office. He was studying Lester's account level sales data when he noticed an interesting pattern. In three of Lester's zip codes there was a hospital account with solid purchases of Marenodiatrome but for the key physician for that hospital there were little or no purchases in the community. This didn't make sense since the product is used in both inpatient and outpatient settings.

Troy found a Xerox copy of the account list in Lester's file with four physician offices with zero purchases where the word "Redfern" was written in red ink in the comment's section.

When Carol brought a flash drive into Troy's office with the sales data for the entire region Troy asked. "Have you ever heard of Redfern?"

"Yes. I've heard the word." Carol said, "Brian used to put meetings in his calendar with that word as the description. Some secret project, I think since he never would let me schedule those meetings for him."

"Are there any files with that word as the subject?" Troy asked.

"I think we sent all of Brian's files back to Boston when he left except for the stack of files we went through when you came on board. Those are in a file box in the storage closet. I haven't had time to ship them back yet."

"Can you bring those to me?" Troy asked.

Carol had opened the storage closet when Patrick and Frank arrived in the lobby of the office.

"Hello, Frank." Carol said, "And I'm guessing you're Patrick?" Carol turned to Patrick and extended her hand.

"Yes." Patrick said, "Thanks for setting things up for us on such short notice."

"No problem at all." Carol answered, "Come this way and I'll show you where I have you set up."

Carol directed the attorneys to the conference room where she had arranged the chairs so that two sat on one side of the conference table and the space for the person being interviewed on the opposite side.

She had also laid out legal pads, pens, markers for the white board and pitchers of water.

"This is excellent." Patrick said, "Great job. Thank you, Carol."

"Would you like some coffee?' Carol offered and without waiting to get an answer already walked down to the break to get a fresh pot, two cups, cream and sugar.

Troy, hearing the voices came down to the conference room to make introductions.

"Nice to meet you Patrick." Troy said and then turned to Frank, "And great seeing you again, Frank."

"You must be really guilty." Patrick said smiling, "Nobody treats attorneys this well."

Troy almost winced at the humor. "I want you to be comfortable. If there's anything you need my office is right down the hall. Otherwise, Carol will help with directing each of the people for your interviews today."

Troy went back to his office and it was only a few minutes later when Carol brought in the file box they had spoken about earlier.

Troy went through the file folders until he found one label in pencil as "Redfern". Opening the file folder, he found a one-page Xerox copy of a Regional account list. 13 accounts with zero purchases had one word in the margin, "Redfern".

Most of the accounts were in Gil's old territory with a few others in Danny's and three in Lester's.

Troy wondered if "Redfern" was some codename for a special project for zero purchase accounts; perhaps a marketing initiative or local sales contest. Since Danny was one of the people being interviewed Troy thought he would ask Danny if he knew what the word "Redfern" meant.

Danny's interview was the first one of the day. He arrived five minutes before his scheduled time of 9am. Troy heard Carol talking to Danny in the lobby.

Troy walked down the hall to greet him.

"Danny" Troy said extending his hand. "Great to see you. How are things going?"

Danny looked stiff and apprehensive.

"I'm fine, I guess." Danny said, "This lawyer stuff is a little unnerving though."

"Relax." Troy said, "Everyone feels that way. I think attorneys make everybody nervous. Patrick and Frank are nice guys, though. You'll be fine."

"Okay" Danny said, still looking anxious.

"Hey, while you're here can I ask you something?" Troy said.

"Sure, what's on your mind?' Danny asked.

"I'm trying to understand more about accounts that don't buy any Marenodiatrome and I keep finding this word 'Redfern'. Does that mean anything to you?" Troy asked

Danny looked as though he had been punched in the stomach. His face suddenly looked pale and he turned to Carol and said, "Where's the rest room?"

Carol pointed down the hall. "First door on the right."

Danny rushed to the rest room appearing to be ill.

When Danny came out of the rest room he was still pale with the front of his hair wet as if he had splashed water on his face. Carol and Troy were still in the lobby area.

"Are you okay for your interview?" Carol asked.

"No. But I'll be right back." Danny said.

Ten minutes passed while Patrick and Frank were beginning to get impatient.

Finally, Danny returned with his computer case. He put the case on the counter along with his phone, his car keys and his name badge.

"I won't be doing any interviews today." Danny said, "I resign."

Danny turned and gave Carol a hug and then briskly walked out the door.

Troy went into the conference room to tell Patrick and Frank what happened.

"That was bizarre." Troy told them, "Danny resigned and said he wasn't going to go through with the interview."

"He resigned?" Patrick said. "That is weird. What happened?"

"It was the strangest thing." Troy began, "I asked him about the word Redfern and he suddenly got sick. He pretty much ran to the rest room. When he came out he excused himself and then brought back his computer, phone and car keys and put them on the counter and told me he was quitting. Just like that."

"You know about Redfern?" Patrick asked.

"I'm trying to find out what it means." Troy said, "I found a list of 13 accounts, all with zero sales with the word Redfern penciled in the comments section. I figured since some of the accounts were in Danny's territory that he might be able to tell me what it is."

"Okay." Patrick said, "I know our interview was scheduled for last, but I think we probably should talk now. Why don't you close the door?"

Troy closed the door as instructed.

"You're sure you've never heard of Redfern before now?" Patrick asked.

"No. Like I told you." Troy said, "I was trying to figure out if there were similarities between low volume territories and I found that there were some zip codes where the hospitals were doing well with Marenodiatrome but the physician offices had no purchases. This seemed weird to me because our product is used both in the hospital and clinic settings. It would seem to me that a physician using the product in one setting would be using it in the other. Then I found this Redfern list and wanted to know whether it was a marketing program or a sales contest or something. I thought Danny might know."

"We can't share the details with you right now, Troy." Patrick said, "But this Redfern thing is pretty much in the middle of this federal investigation. Danny's computer was the one with some deleted files. We can't be sure, but we think the files were related to Redfern. At this point I need you to do two things. First, don't talk to anyone about Redfern without talking to me first."

"Okay." Troy said.

"Second, stop doing any more investigation on your own relative to Redfern."

"Okay" Troy said again.

"And one last thing." Patrick said, "Whatever you already have on Redfern give to me today."

"You've got it Patrick." Troy said.

"Okay." Patrick said, "We're finished with you. You can go back to work."

As soon as Troy left the conference room, Patrick turned to Frank.

"You think we can trust this guy?" Patrick asked.

"Yes, I do." Frank said. "I trust him for two reasons. He was quite forthcoming with the internal expense audit situation and of course, he's too new to have been involved in the Redfern thing."

While the attorneys could not share what was going on in the investigation, it was shaping up to be an event that could dramatically impact the future of the company. The attorneys knew some information about this emerging scandal.

Marenodiatrome is a product that is used to support the structure of tissue during surgical procedures. Mareno makes the product in one size to accommodate a wide range of needs during surgery. Payers pay the full $5000 product price for each procedure regardless of how much of the product is needed during a procedure. The unused portion of the product is medical waste.

Redfern was a repackaging company that took the remaining unused Marenodiatrome product not used in a hospital procedure, repackaged it to look like original product and sold it to physicians. They had a sophisticated scheme that involved charging full price then giving a heavily rebated discount back to the physician.

Since payers pay for the full product rather than what is used for the procedure payers were providing full reimbursement for product that cost the physicians less than half price while Redfern paid virtually nothing for the product because it was waste from other procedures. Each physician had proof that they had purchased "original" Marenodiatrome from Redfern in the form of a proper invoice, lot number and bar code in case they were audited. The rebates were processed under another name, Kadence Collection Service, a subsidiary of Redfern and totally disassociated from the product. In the meantime, Redfern made millions.

Redfern paid low level hospital employees to save the product for Redfern to pick up, telling them that the product was being recovered to use for charitable purposes in third world countries. They paid these employees with virtually no paper trail by providing them gift cards although some employees collected the product waste without accepting any payment.

The attorneys had obviously put much of this together through document searches in cooperation with federal authorities. They suspected that Redfern was created and owned by a handful of Mareno Bioscience employees. Now the only real questions that needed to be answered were who within Mareno was involved and to what extent.

The interviews with Cindy, Sammy and Carol seemed to go well. Each of them came out of the ninety-minute sessions looking no worse for the conversations. While the whole Redfern issue remained in Troy's mind, he also knew that he should leave it alone for now. Instead, he continued to concentrate on next week's work sessions.

Late in the day Troy called Buzz to touch base and ask a couple of questions about the computer program Mareno used for video-conferencing.

Buzz answered in the phone with his normal, friendly manner.

"Troy, Bud." Buzz said, "How are you doing with the looney bin?'

"It's full on, for sure." Troy said.

"Still drinking from the firehose?" Buzz said laughing, referring to his comment he made a few weeks prior.

"Yeah, but I haven't drowned yet." Troy said chuckling.

"Well Bud, what's on your mind?" Buzz asked.

"I'm getting ready to schedule a video conference and wanted to ask about the software program we use." Troy stated.

"And what would make you think I know a thing about that?" Buzz said with a hearty laugh. "When it comes to technology I defer to my trusted administrative associate. Now ask me about people; now that I might be of some value."

"Fair enough." Troy said, "I could use some help there too. I've got a work session with a low performer and a high performer next week. I'm not sure how each will adapt to my management style."

"Your what?" Buzz said with a laugh.

"My management style." Troy reiterated.

"Okay, I'll bite." Buzz said, "Tell me about your management style."

"Well, I believe that our job as managers is to bring out

the best in people." Troy began. "To do that, I think a manager should always be very collaborative and open. I think we should do more listening than talking. I think we should help others to find solutions to problems rather than providing solutions."

"Dude, who am I talking to, Dale Carnegie?" Buzz said laughing. "You've been reading too many books."

"Well, what style of management do you prefer?" Troy said defensively.

"That's easy." Buzz said, "Whatever style works. You need to understand something, Troy. No one cares about your management style. Your style should depend totally on who you're trying to coach. They aren't going to adapt to your style; you have to adapt to theirs."

"That makes it sound like I should treat some people differently than others." Troy said, "That doesn't sound fair."

"Different doesn't mean unfair." Buzz said, "Different means using the right tool in the old tool box."

"I'm not following." Troy said.

"Look, think of it this way." Buzz said, "You have a managerial tool box and it has all kinds of tools. For example, positive reinforcement is one of those tools."

"Okay." Troy said.

"What are some of the others?" Buzz asked.

"Criticism?" Troy asked.

"Sure." Buzz said, "But also direction, challenging, teaching, motivating, even score-keeping."

"Okay, I think I see what you're saying." Troy said pensively.

"Let me tell you with any team of people you're going to

have different skill levels. You may have one or two outstanding performers. Then maybe a few above average performers and lots of middle performers. Unfortunately, you will probably have one or two poor performers and maybe a couple of newbies." Buzz observed.

"That pretty much describes my team." Troy acknowledged.

"What I'm suggesting is that all of those different skill levels require a different primary management tool. I've got to tell you a story. When I first became a manager, I had ten people reporting to me. I loved to write memos back in those days. I wrote a memo to the team at least once a week. One day I'm talking to Sam and he asks why I wrote so many memos. I told him I wrote memos so everyone has the same direction. Do know what he told me?"

"No, but I bet it's good." Troy said.

"He says, when you write a memo to the team to give direction, the top two or three people are thinking, 'does he think I'm an idiot?' the people at the bottom are thinking, 'what the devil is he talking about', only the middle guys are going to appreciate the memo. He says to me 'make life easier on yourself, just give the middle performers a call'." Buzz said laughing.

"That oversimplifies but I guess he had a point." Troy acknowledged.

"Think about the primary managerial tool that is needed for middle performers." Buzz said.

"I guess Sam would say that direction is what they need most?" Troy asked.

"Pretty much." Buzz said, "And what about the newbie?"

"I guess the primary tool would be teaching." Troy said.

"And the above average performer?" Buzz asked.

"Maybe motivation or positive reinforcement?" Troy asked.

"What about the outstanding performer?" Buzz asked.

"Again, I'd say positive reinforcement." Troy said.

"Not so fast." Buzz said. "These guys at the top are really good and they have ego's that are as big as their bonuses. Positive reinforcement really only matters if it comes from someone they really respect and then only if the achievement recognized is truly exceptional."

"Really?" Troy said skeptically.

"Think about it." Buzz said, "What if I complemented you on the correctness of your grammar. Would that make you feel good?"

"Probably not." Troy answered, "I'd figure, doesn't everyone in our jobs use good grammar?"

"Exactly." Buzz said, "And what if the compliment came from someone who was totally uneducated?

"Then the compliment would mean nothing at all." Troy said.

"Some of our top performers know they're good and they probably think they're better at their jobs than we were…and they might be right." Buzz said.

"What do you think the best managerial tool is for the exceptional performer?" Troy asked.

"I've found that challenging them is often what they respond to." Buzz answered. "Let me give you an example. I've got this sales rep, Margo who has won President's Cup seven times."

"Yes, I met her on the President's Cup trip this year." Troy said.

"Last year I sat down with Margo and told her that even though she already had the highest growth in the country at 34% I wondered if anyone could top 40%. I told her that I had done the math and thought it was probably impossible." Buzz said. "What do you think she did?'

"I'm guessing she topped 40%." Troy said.

"The art of challenging a top performer." Buzz said.

"You haven't talked about the low performer." Troy said, still skeptical about the whole managerial tool box idea.

"Well, let's make some assumptions." Buzz said, "Let's assume you've already done everything possible to help the low performer. You've made a good diagnosis, you've tried to teach and coach. Nothing is working."

"Okay, then what?" Troy asked.

"Then, I become a score-keeper." Buzz said, "I essentially set the mark that needs to be achieved and I sit back and keep score."

"I can't believe that HR could embrace that." Troy said with skepticism.

"Well, my point is this." Buzz said, "If you find that you want the person to succeed more than they want to succeed, you have the wrong person in the job. I try to help that person find a better match for them."

"You're talking 'will' versus 'skill'?" Troy asked.

"Yes." Buzz said, "And that's another way to think of which managerial tool to pull out of the tool box. I like to think of 'will' and 'skill' on two different axes. If the person has will but no skill, it is your job to teach."

"That, I understand." Troy said more enthusiastically.

"If the person has both will and skill, you could provide positive reinforcement or challenge." Buzz said.

"If you have skill but no will, you probably need to motivate or provide pretty firm direction." Troy said excitedly.

"But no will and no skill?" Buzz observed, "then I have no time."

"That's cold." Troy said.

"No. That's practical." Buzz said, "Any way you look at this, the main point is that this has very little to do with your management style and everything to do with what each person needs. There's no magic bullet, here. If you have twelve people you need to be fair with all of them but different in how you manage each of them."

"Fair enough." Troy acknowledged, "Lesson learned."

"Changing the subject…" Buzz said, "How are your vacancies coming along?"

"Well, I hired the Duke MBA that Sam put in front of me for North Georgia." Troy said.

"Is she working out?" Buzz asked.

"Actually, I think she's going to be okay." Troy said, "She only needs a little more help at the beginning."

"What about the other two vacancies?" Buzz asked.

"Now I have three." Troy said, "Danny quit this morning."

"Wow, they're dropping like flies." Buzz said with a laugh. "Don't scare them all away with your managerial style."

"Funny as a heart attack." Troy said, "I'm down to two candidates for one of the positions and I'm having human resources work up a package for the other. Now I've got to get started trying to fill Danny's territory."

Buzz laughed, "How difficult can it be to find someone to live in Gainesville going into the winter? Try getting someone to live in Buffalo."

"Yeah, you're right." Troy said, "It could be worse."

"Without a doubt." Buzz said continuing to laugh.

"Listen, Buzz." Troy said closing the conversation, "I really appreciate your insights about adjusting my style to meet the needs of my team members. I'm sure they will appreciate too."

"Troy, you're really a good guy." Buzz said, "You are open which makes you a good learner, but you have good instincts, too. Don't be too moved by what others say or by what you read. You really will find out what works for you in time."

"Thanks, Buzz." Troy said, "Have a good evening."

QUESTIONS TO CONSIDER

1) What do you tell others when they ask about your management style?

2) How do you determine whether poor performance is due to "will" or "skill"?

3) How would a federal investigation impact the way you manage day-to-day?

4) What "tools" from the "managerial toolbox" do you tend to overuse?

CHAPTER FOURTEEN: THE STAR OPPORTUNITY

The weeks following the initial attorney visits seemed a blur to Troy. The training program for the new companion product for Marenodiatrome was in full swing meaning that in addition to the normal field days Troy also had to put on state-by-state training meetings on Fridays.

Rather than cut into his field schedule, Troy compromised on his administrative days which meant that the burden of paperwork was almost overwhelming. Troy often stayed up well after midnight to keep everything in line. Troy's ideal of Dennis's "Life's Pie" seemed like some vision of paradise; well outside of Troy's ability to achieve. Heather noticed.

"I can't begin to tell you how much I miss you when you're on the road." Heather said. "And sometimes when you are here, you're in your office until I fall asleep. Mom and Dad are always asking when we're going to have a baby. I'm pretty sure you have to be around to make that happen."

"I know, I thought this would be temporary." Troy assured her, "I know it's become a regular thing."

"You keep telling me to relax; that it will get better" Heather said, "But you've been saying that for months. Next week is Thanksgiving. You plan to be home for that?"

Troy was slow answering. "Of course, I'm home for Thanksgiving." he said.

"But let me guess..." Heather said, "You'll have to travel

on the Sunday after Thanksgiving."

Troy took a deep breath. "Yes. That's true." He said, "But the manager's meeting is in Phoenix and I won't have to leave until later in the afternoon."

Heather rolled her eyes and went into the other room.

Troy sat in the living room and put his face in his hands. He considered following Heather but thought it better to give her some space. He wondered if it really would get better. He knew Heather was right. Things hadn't slowed down one bit. If anything, with the new product and the federal investigation it had gotten worse. Then Troy thought about the meeting after Thanksgiving. This was the final business plan update for the year with Sam and the regional directors.

Troy was proud of what had been accomplished in the southeast. Business was turning around much faster than he would have anticipated. It looked as though his region might finish third of the six regions; a big turnaround from being in dead last.

Troy had made some impressive hires thanks to guidance from Buzz and Greta. All in all, Troy expected the coming year to be one where the southeast could easily rise to prominence. When it came to his work at Mareno, things really couldn't be better.

Then there was his personal life. True to Dennis' warnings about new managers letting work gobble up the other pieces of "Life's Pie", Troy seemed to do nothing but work. Heather joined a church, started a new job, had become friends with two neighborhood women and even joined a tennis league. In January, she would start her MSN program.

Troy, in contrast, had been to church twice, had played

one round of golf and the closest to new friends he could claim were the workers at the Delta Crown Room at the airport. The bike Troy used to ride logging over 50 miles per week in Cleveland hadn't come out of the garage in Atlanta.

Troy went into the master bedroom and found Heather calm and resting.

He sat on the side of the bed and leaned over to kiss the back of her neck. "I'm sorry, Angel." Troy said, "I've let this job take me over. I don't know how but I've got to make some changes. This job is bigger than I anticipated. Dennis has warned me over and over about Life's Pie, but I can't seem to find a way to keep everything balanced."

Heather rolled over and put her arms around Troy's neck. He held her close to him. They both realized that something positive was going to happen to get life back in balance.

Troy once again thought about his life and the balance of his priorities. He realized that his addiction to career was like a drug he could not do without but could only find a way to intelligently manage; a wild beast that he must harness to ride to success without letting it devour him. Troy wasn't sure yet what to do differently but he knew that he had to change.

The next morning Troy was waiting for Heather at the breakfast table with two pieces of paper.

"Good morning, Sweetheart." Troy said as he poured Heather some coffee. "I have a task that I think will help us manage the balance in our life."

Heather smiled, "I'm game."

"I've written the following categories on each paper; fun, work, spirituality, relationships, community and other" Troy said, "I want each of us to write out the two or three things we could do in a year that would make us feel successful with each category. Let's do it separately and then see what each other have written".

Heather and Troy took the exercise seriously and after a few minutes were ready to share.

	Heather	Troy
Fun	1)take a 7-day cruise 2)have a date night every Saturday 3)take up painting	1)take a vacation 2)take a day trip every month
Work	1)change to part time work 2)start my MSN program	1)take every Friday as office day 2)work from home twice per month 3)become #1 team in company
Spirituality	1)go to church every week 2)Bible study once a week 3)read a new book once a month	1)go to church on all special occasions 2)read 20 new books
Relationships	1)visit Mom and Dad 3 times	1)have a date night once a month with Heather
Community	1)work at the food pantry	1)join Kiwanis Club
Other	1)start planning for a family	

When they had finished their goals Heather and Troy were surprised at some of the things on each other's lists.

"I didn't know you wanted to take a cruise." Troy said, "We need to schedule something right away. We both need a vacation."

"I can't believe you want to have a date night, too!" Heather noted, "I want one every week and you want one once a month."

"Looks like maybe we need to plan on at least twice monthly" Troy acknowledged.

"Troy, this was a great idea." Heather said, "It really helps clarify what's important to both of us."

"Yeah, I'm hoping this will help me focus on the right priorities." Troy said.

"It's certainly a step in the right direction" Heather said with a smile.

"I'm glad its soon Thanksgiving. "Troy said, "It will give us a few days to spend together".

Thanksgiving came at a great time for Troy. He needed a few days away from the job. In a move that surprised Heather, Troy cancelled his field days and instead spent Monday and Tuesday of the holiday week preparing for the Business Plan update. He emerged from his office at 4pm on Tuesday evening as Heather was coming home from her nursing shift.

Troy met her as she came into the kitchen from the garage. He put his arms around her and held her close.

"You're off for the rest of the week, right?" Troy asked.

"Yes." Heather confirmed, "Why?"

"Because, we are going to have a traditional Thanksgiving dinner in our own home on Thursday. Let's call your Mom and Dad. Let's get them plane tickets and we won't take no for an answer." Troy said.

Heather didn't hesitate. "She immediately called her parents and made the arrangements. And true to form, she wouldn't allow excuses. They would be coming to Atlanta Hartsfield on Thursday morning...using frequent flyer points and some of the additional credit limit Troy had recently added to the Gold Card.

"Sometimes, I think we have to splurge a bit. You and I are both making good money. Even though it has been tight recently, our finances should settle back in place after the holidays." Troy said, fully enjoying the look of happiness on his wife's face.

Troy spent the next few days enjoying the holiday. Heather's mom and dad were truly appreciative of the trip and the chance to see their daughter's new home. They even seemed proud of Troy.

When Sunday arrived, Troy didn't mind leaving for Phoenix. He felt rested for the first time in months and more importantly, he knew he was well-prepared for the business plan update.

Even though it was still early evening Phoenix time when Troy arrived at the Scottsdale Princess, he didn't look for the other regional managers but rather went to his room and watched the end of the Cleveland/Arizona football game. He wanted solitude and to be completely relaxed for the next morning's session.

When Sam gathered with the regional managers the

following morning he demonstrated his normal charisma.

"Troy, where were you last night?' Sam asked, "I left a message on your phone. We all went out for barbeque last night. You should have been there."

"Yes, I know." Troy said, "I was beat after the holiday, so I sat down on the bed and the next thing you know I fell asleep in my room. By the time I got your message, I'm sure the whole thing was over."

Immediately, Troy felt guilty making up a story. The truth was he wanted to be alone last night. It's not like anybody really cares. Why lie about it?

"Well, don't stand us up tonight; we're going to the Capital Grill." Sam said with a smile.

"I wouldn't miss it." Troy said with enthusiasm.
Sam opened the meeting with slides about company performance.

"Fourth quarter looks amazing." Sam said enthusiastically, "All of you have really picked up your game but I have to give special props to Troy. His group has been on fire, leading the company in percentage growth. The southeast region has moved into third place from dead last. I want to start with Troy's business plan update so that maybe we can all learn some things to turn up the heat on our overall performance."

While Sam spoke, Troy looked around the room at his colleagues. Linh looked proud. Jim looked bored. Cheryl smiled as if hearing a mildly entertaining story. Scott looked angry. Really angry. Troy had no time to think why his peers were reacting in different ways because Sam called him to the front to share his plan update.

As Troy pulled up his first slide, he looked around the

room. "The first thing I want to say is that while I'm pleased that the southeast isn't lagging behind in everything I know that it is far easier to show growth from the bottom of the pack. In addition, I am still trying to sort out the challenges within the region. If it hadn't been for all of you helping me over the past few months I don't know how I could've done this job."

Linh, Cheryl, Buzz, Jim and the others shook their heads in appreciation. Scott showed no emotion.

"On this first slide, let me show you our growth and where it is coming from.

"I can tell you where it's coming from." Scott said sarcastically, "One word...Redfern."

Troy looked at Scott and smiled. "As you probably know, Redfern is a topic that I have been told by the attorneys that we are not supposed to talk about but Scott, you are right, whatever Redfern was, the territories that were part of it are now showing exceptional growth."

Troy turned to the next slide and showed his business plan giving credit to Jim and Alex for their help in crafting the plan.

"You know, thanks to Alex and Jim's guidance" Troy said, "I think this is the first business plan that I've followed and used daily. Every work session starts with a discussion of the plan."

"Wonder where you got that idea?" Scott said with a scowl.

"You're right, Scott." Troy said, "You really were enormously helpful with your ideas on work session planning. That helped a lot."

Despite Troy's obvious attempts to appease Scott, the snipes and comments continued throughout Troy's presentation. The other regional managers began to compensate by reinforcing the points Troy was making. It was clear that Scott was peeved about something, but Troy obviously couldn't address it in front of the group.

Troy then went to his roster and showed the initial work plan he had designed with Cheryl to prioritize his coaching days and to help him select the right "What" to coach each person. Once again Troy gave honor to Cheryl for her help.

Troy then talked about his recruiting strategy and the help that Buzz and Greta had been in helping him select some great new sales representatives.

"Yeah, it helps when you get blue-ribbon candidates handed to you on a silver platter from Sam's office." Scott said under his breath.

Finally, Troy completed his business plan presentation and began to answer questions. Even though Troy was only about a year into the manager's job, it was clear that the lessons he had learned from the others had helped him achieve a great deal. The team applauded after Troy's presentation except for Scott who excused himself for a restroom break.

"Troy," Sam said in front of the group, "You've really made a lot a progress in a short amount of time. Keep up the good work."

During a break Troy consulted Linh about the tension with Scott.

"I don't know what I did to upset Scott." Troy said, "Honestly, I didn't know how to respond."

Linh smiled, "Troy, you responded exactly as you should have. You took the high road and as a result, Scott looked foolish. If you noticed, everyone was aligning with you."

"I felt like I was the foolish one, taking his abuse." Troy answered.

"Look, there will always be guys like Scott around." Linh said, "They like to try to bully others. I've seen it often over the years. The thing is these guys almost always self-destruct. Oh, there are some that get promoted but sooner or later they fail. You handled things beautifully. Well done."

"I hope you're right." Troy said returning to the meeting room.

The rest of the day went well with Troy, Buzz and Cheryl all presenting their updates. Scott, Linh would present the next day.

Sam adjourned the regional managers and then took out his phone to make a call.

"Troy." Sam whispered, "Hang back. I've got to make a call, but it will be short. I want to talk to you."

Troy figured that Sam was going to ask about the tension with Scott. Despite Linh's counsel Troy went over in his mind what he could have done differently. Then, he allowed his emotions to run wild. "What's with this guy, anyway?" Troy thought, "Obviously, he wanted to make me look bad, but why?"

The more Troy thought about it the more frustrated he became. He had worked himself into an irritated state by the time Sam motioned for him to sit down.

"Sorry for the phone call." Sam said, "There's something I want to talk to you about."

"I know." Troy said, "But what could I have done when one of my colleagues is acting like a jerk? I was trying to play it cool but damn, it pissed me off."

"What in the Hell are you talking about?" Sam asked

"Scott." Troy said, "He was undermining everything I said today."

"Oh, for God sakes Troy you sound like a little girl." Sam said with irritation, "Don't talk to me about this kind of stuff. Manage it."

"Sorry. I thought that's what you wanted to talk to me about." Troy said defeated.

"Not even close." Sam said, "And it disappoints me that you even let that kind of thing bother you. Kids need to learn how to play in the sandbox together. Now, get over it."

"Okay." Troy said with his head bent, "Sorry."

"Troy, there's going to be changes around here." Sam said quietly.

"Okay." Troy said.

"I wanted to tell you up front because it could impact you in a big way." Sam said.

"That sounds kind of ominous." Troy said.

"Yeah." Sam acknowledged, "Or it could be the biggest opportunity you have ever experienced in your life."

"Why? What's going on?" Troy asked.

"Can't tell you all the details." Sam said, "but how would you feel about an overseas assignment?'

"Where?" Troy asked.

Not sure yet." Sam answered, "Maybe Belgium. Maybe London, Maybe Singapore."

"I'm not sure. It's sounds really exciting." Troy said, "of course I'd have to see how Heather feels. I mean we only recently got settled in Atlanta. And I do love the regional manager role."

"That's the thing. That role is going to change. There will be new titles, more structure and less autonomy after the changes go through. And there's no guarantee that you'd stay in Atlanta."

"Are you kidding?" Troy said in shock.

"I need to be able to trust you right now." Sam said,

"There are only three people that know about this and you are the fourth. If anything leaks, I will know it came from you."

"You can trust me." Troy said, "I promise."

"In the next week we will be making some announcements. We're going to be bought out by a bigger company. Our president is retiring. I'll be taking on a completely new assignment. The regions will be replaced by something like 12 districts. The whole organization will expand but the new company will fill most of the jobs with their own people. There will be two sales leads, one for the west and one for the east. You haven't been around for long enough to get one of those jobs, but ex-US is a whole different thing. Our buy-out partner has little presence in Europe and Asia and they've put me in charge of everything outside of North America. I can take anyone at Moreno with me; whomever I want."

"And you want me?" Troy asked.

"Yes, if you can stop getting your shorts in a wad over a few jealous comments from a colleague." Sam said with a smile.

"I would absolutely love to go!" Troy said with excitement.

"Where?" Sam said.

"Anywhere you want to send me." Troy said

"And Heather?" Sam asked

"That could be another issue. I will try to convince her." Troy said knowing that he was overcommitting.

"I'm sure you will." Sam said putting his arm around Troy and patting his shoulder.

"Are any of the other regional managers going to follow you overseas?" Troy asked.

"You ask too many questions when all I want is one answer." Sam said, "Get on the phone with Heather and confirm that you will go with me to international."

Sam walked out of the room but turned again to Troy.

"Remember; tell no one about this other than Heather." Sam said emphatically. "We have to keep this under our hats until markets open tomorrow morning."

"I thought it wasn't going to come out for a week?" Troy said.

"All the internal stuff will be settled over the next week." Sam said, "The announcement of the buy-out will come at market's opening tomorrow. Get a good night's sleep."

"What about our dinner at the Capital Grill?" Troy asked.

"Oh yeah. Forgot." Sam answered, "I'll see you at seven. Remember, not a single word."

QUESTIONS TO CONSIDER

1) How have you learned to completely turn away from work during personal time?

2) Troy felt confident on his presentation because he reserved time for preparation? What steps do you take before making a presentation to ensure success?

3) If you were Troy what would you consider helping decide between opportunities?

4) Could you be trusted not to share the information Sam provided for 24 hours? What about a week?

5) How would you handle such a big opportunity regarding the impact it might have on your family?

CHAPTER FIFTEEN: THE STAR NEWS

Troy went back to his room and sat on the bed. He wondered how to break this unexpected news to Heather. There's no doubt that she been open to changes in the past. Yet this time there were many questions and few answers. An international assignment, but where? Would they have to learn a new language? What would be Troy's new title? Exactly what would he be doing?

It almost seemed foolish to approach Heather with this new opportunity when he had so little information. Yet, Troy trusted Sam. Considering the big changes at Mareno in the states Troy could easily get lost in the shuffle if he decided to stay in the domestic organization. Moving to Europe or Asia seemed exotic and exciting. This was more than a simple career opportunity. It truly was an opportunity of a lifetime.

If only he could tell Heather in person rather than by phone. He was sure that if they could talk face-to-face that she would agree that this was an opportunity that they must take. Yet this came so soon; she had only begun to get comfortable in Atlanta.

Troy thought about how to present the opportunity to Heather. He rehearsed his "presentation" in front of the mirror by the desk. He wanted to sound confident, positive and enthusiastic. He wanted to emphasize how much this would mean to their marriage, how they could see new places and experience many new things together.

Troy took a deep breath before hitting Heather's picture on speed dial on his cell phone. She answered right away.

"Troy, I am glad you called." Heather said with an uncharacteristically bubbly voice.

"Hi Babe." Troy answered. "I miss you and I would much rather be with you right now, but I have some news that can't wait."

"Me too." Heather said enthusiastically "I couldn't wait for you to call."

"Really?" Troy said, "Well, what's your news?"

"No, you go first." Heather said.

"Are you sure?" Troy answered, "You sound pretty excited."

"Thrilled, actually." Heather said, "But go ahead, tell me your news first."

"Okay." Troy said, "You know how we've always loved to travel but haven't always had enough money to go to some of our most dreamed about locations?"

"Yes." Heather answered.

"Well, I've been asked to take an international assignment." Troy said bursting with enthusiasm.

Silence. It was as if Heather was a balloon that suddenly was completely deflated.

"Babe, did you hear me?" Troy asked tentatively

"Yes." Heather said almost dejectedly, "It sounds like you're pretty excited. Where do they want us to go?"

"Are you okay?" Troy asked, "You sound like you're really disappointed."

"No, I'm fine." Heather said sounding anything but fine. "Where do they want to send us?"

"I'm not sure yet. Maybe Belgium or even Singapore. I think we will have some say in the matter." Troy said.

"You don't even know where we would be living?" Heather said with shock. "You expect me to be excited about going somewhere halfway across the world and not even know where?"

"No. I totally get it." Troy said, "This is by far the biggest decision we will ever have to make together, and I have so little information. I know it is hard for you to get excited before all that falls into place. Sam told me about some major changes in the company. If I go international, it will be a huge promotion for us. If I stay here I may even get a demotion and we might not get to stay in Atlanta. This is all a whirlwind and we will have to work through it as we get more information."

"Does Sam expect us to make a commitment like today? Without even knowing any details?" Heather asked.

"You know Sam." Troy said apologetically, "Can I at least tell him that we are open to the possibility?"

"That's a big ask, particularly with the news I was anxious to tell you." Heather answered calmly but dejectedly.

"Oh yes. What news is that?" Troy asked.

"Troy, *my* news." Heather said, "Is that I'm pregnant. We are going to have a baby."

"A baby?" Troy said more as a statement than a question. "Wow, that is fantastic."

"Really?" Heather said, "So you're okay with it?"

"I'm thrilled!" Troy said enthusiastically "We are amazingly blessed. We are like one of those couples everyone envies. We have it all."

"Yes. I guess we do." Heather affirmed.

"Your news is so much better than mine." Troy said, "Wow. This really takes things to a completely different level.

I'm going to be a Dad."

"The only thing is..." Heather observed, "Surely, we can't consider the international thing now."

Troy sat in silence for a moment.

"No." Troy said dejectedly, "I guess that taking our son or daughter overseas would be too big of a risk."

"You don't sound convincing." Heather answered, "You really want to do this thing anyway, don't you?"

"I don't know." Troy answered, "You are the most important thing in my life. I want what's best for us. Still, this international thing is intriguing. I will be happy doing whatever is best for us, but could we at least consider it. Is that fair?"

"Yes. That's fair." Heather answered, "But I won't make any promises."

"I appreciate that." Troy said, "And thanks you for at least being open to the possibility. I'll put Sam off for now until we have time to discuss this live."

"I love you, Troy." Heather said genuinely.

"That goes double for you." Troy said. "I'll call you tomorrow."

Troy hung up the phone. He undressed and got in the shower. As the warm water washed over his body Troy settled into the new information that first, he was going to be a father and second, that he might soon be living in an exciting location for an opportunity that might never come again.

A few hours later the regional managers met in the lobby for their dinner at Capital Grill.

Sam acted cool as a cucumber for the entire dinner until the group went out to the stretch limo waiting outside the restaurant.

He leaned over to Troy and asked. "What did Heather have to say?"

"Can we talk privately when we get back to the hotel?" Troy asked.

"Of course." Sam answered before returning his attention to the entire group once everyone had settled in the stretch limo. "Thank you, folks for sharing this evening with me. Let's have one more toast. Here's to this incredible group of regional managers. I appreciate you and maybe this is the scotch talking, but I want you to know that I love you guys. No matter what changes take place in our lives or in this company you will always have my admiration and my love."

The admiration was clearly mutual as the group returned their praise of Sam. For Troy, having inside information of the impending changes, the trip back to the hotel was a long one. While he wanted to please Heather, he had built a special connection with his mentor, Sam. The thought of disappointing Sam was nearly as strong as the compulsion to please Heather.

When they arrived at the hotel Sam said goodnight to the group and motioned to Troy to join him in the lounge.

"What was Heather's reaction to the international assignment?" Sam asked.

"Well, she kind of upstaged me, Sam." Troy said with a smile.

"How so?" Sam answered.

"She told me that she was pregnant." Troy said proudly.

"Well, isn't that like a woman?" Sam laughed, "They will do anything to be the center of attention. How do you feel about that?"

"It is amazing to think that I will be a father." Troy answered enthusiastically, ignoring another of Sam's misogynist comments.

"And a very successful father at that." Sam answered, "Do you know what an international assignment will do for your career? You will be one of a handful of people that have run businesses in other parts of the world. Your personal worth will be high whether you continue to move up in our current organization or to go to another multi-national corporation. "Truly, the world is your oyster, Troy."

"Sam, having a child changes everything for both of us." Troy said, "I'm really not sure I can get Heather to go along."

"I'm not surprised." Sam said, "Janay wasn't a fan at first either. Now she is totally on board. I think maybe Janay and I need to make a quick trip to Atlanta to take you and Heather to dinner."

"That would be wonderful." Troy said. "When?"

"As soon as this meeting is over." Sam answered, "I'll fly back with you and have Janay meet us there."

Following the business plan update meeting Sam and Troy flew first class back to Atlanta thanks to some frequent flyer benefits Sam had accumulated.

"I've got more details to share with you now, Troy." Sam stated, "If you decide to accept the assignment I'm going to name you Executive Director of Asia-Pacific. I know that sounds crazy, but the new company was more than ready to give up such titles. I will be President of EAA."

"EAA?" Troy asked.

"Europe, Asia and Africa" Sam answered, "Essentially, the

whole world outside of North and South America."

"That's impressive." Troy answered.

"It would be except we have precious little business outside of the states." Sam said, "We will have to build the business from scratch. We have 24 months to generate sales in our geography.

I need you to be able to commit. I can't do this without you."

"Let's say Heather goes along." Troy asked, "What does the package look like?"

"You certainly cut right to the chase, don't you?" Sam said with a laugh, "Troy, you're going to like this. I think the ideal location for you is Hong Kong. We will provide a 50% increase in salary, increase your stock options by 75%; we will pay for your housing and provide you a private car with driver. Heather will also have domestic help."

"Are you kidding?" Troy asked shocked.

"And the first $100,000 is pretty much tax free as an expatriate." Sam said enthusiastically, "If you plan properly, you and Heather can be set financially when your 24-month assignment is over."

"What do I do when the assignment is over?" Troy asked.

"Troy, you're going to be building an entire business in Asia. If you're still with Mareno they will guarantee a job and salary at least the level you were at before taking the assignment." Sam answered, "But other companies are always hungry for executives with international experience. You will pretty much be able to write your own ticket."

"That sounds great." Troy said, "What about Heather?"

"She will live in luxury in one of the best countries in the world, have a chauffeur take her anywhere she wants to go and pretty much live the life of a diva." Sam answered. "What's missing here? She's going to love it...and you for taking her there. If you think about it, she probably will want to stay home with the baby for a while anyway. This gives her the perfect opportunity to do so."

The plane soon landed in Atlanta and Sam decided to send a car later that day to pick up Heather and Troy to take them to a quaint place north of the city called Chateau Elan. This French-styled hotel, spa and winery was the perfect location to discuss the exotic assignment Sam had in mind for Troy.

Sam and Janay met Troy and Heather in the fine French dining room that could easily be mistaken for one of the finest Parisian restaurants.

Over a bottle of Merlot, only a few sips of which Heather would allow herself as a newly pregnant woman, the four talked about the baby, the future of Europe and Asia and the critical role that both Sam and Troy would play in the amazing success of the company. At the end of the evening, Heather and Troy went to their hotel suite which was uniquely situated in the middle of the spa. They put on their robes and walked down to a sensual couple's massage. In the middle of the massage, Heather raised her head from the massage table and spoke to Troy.

"Baby, I want you to know." Heather said lovingly, "I'm in. Where ever you go, whatever you do, I love you and I'll follow you. Let's go to Hong Kong and have our baby."

No sweeter words had Troy ever heard.

QUESTIONS TO CONSIDER:

1) If an opportunity came to go to a new country would you go?

2) What are the risks and benefits of taking on a new, unexpected assignment?

3) When confronted with a new opportunity what rules do you follow to make sure your decision is right for both you and your family?

CHAPTER SIXTEEN: WELCOME TO HONG KONG

Troy was in his Atlanta office early the following Monday. It was a bright December morning when the news broke on CNN. Minutes later his office was flooded with phone calls.

The first wave of news was that Mareno Biosciences had been purchased by the well-renowned German medical device company, McManus Medical. McManus' Vice Chairman of the Board, a scrappy young industrialist named Helmut Heilderschmidt had been named President of the new company which would be called McManus-Mareno Health. In the initial press conference Heilderschmidt promised to make the operation in the United States one of premier sales and marketing status. He also announced a commercialization initiative in Europe and Asia that within 24 months would be the third most productive healthcare company in both regions.

In the press conference Heilderschmidt acknowledged that Mareno Biosciences had been the target of a whistle-blower federal lawsuit which had been settled with the government during negotiations for the purchase of Mareno. He said that because of the investigation brought on by the lawsuit, McManus-Mareno Health had removed several key executives as well as some lower level employees and would hold themselves to a much higher standard in the future.

Heilderschmidt also had praises for the former Vice President of Mareno Biosciences, Sam Logan who would now lead up operations in Europe, Asia and Africa. Two Executive Directors were also named for the international operation, Cheryl Masters for Europe and Troy Noble, for Asia-Pacific.

The first call Troy received was from Dennis.

"Congratulations, my friend." Dennis said through the cell phone.

"Thanks Dennis." Troy said, "But it sounds like a much bigger deal than it is. Right now, I'm pretty much Executive Director of myself. I'm not even sure where to begin but I'll have a few people who are already in place that can help me get started."

"How's Heather feeling about things?" Dennis asked.

"She's on board but she has a lot of anxiety about the move to Hong Kong." Troy answered honestly.

"Her life is really being turned upside down." Dennis said, "I heard she was pregnant."

"Yes." Troy said, "And that's a whole different thing for both of us."

"Now Life's Pie is more important than ever." Dennis said, "What are you going to do to help Heather adjust?"

"I hadn't thought about it." Troy said, "Why, do you have some suggestions?"

"Absolutely." Dennis answered. "First, you need to recognize that Hong Kong is far different culturally than the States. The company offers cross-cultural training and you both need to go."

"I had no idea." Troy said, "That sounds great."

"Have you ever heard of transitional depression?" Dennis continued.

"No, not really." Troy answered.

"It is not at all unusual for the trailing spouse to experience a real down period after the move. At first, the spouse is excited. They get to find a new house and get new things. Everything is an adventure. But while the executive has a support system around them at work immediately, the spouse has to re-establish every aspect of his or her life…even something as simple as knowing where the grocery store is located or how to find a new place to work out."

"Yes, Heather definitely experienced that in Atlanta." Troy said. "For a while she stayed on the sofa in her pajamas all day."

"That was probably transitional depression." Dennis said, "Expect that it will be ten times more difficult in Hong Kong. Having the baby might help but it could also make her feel more isolated."

"That's a discouraging thought." Troy acknowledged.

"Psychologists understand this phenomenon and can help someone through." Dennis said.

"A Psychologist?" Troy said, "Really?"

"Troy, for someone who is so smart, you're really missing the point here." Dennis said with a chuckle, "Going to a psychologist helps someone make the transition. It doesn't mean there's anything wrong with them. Not only that but the company has an employee assistance program that will handle all the details for you."

"I hadn't even thought of that." Troy acknowledged, "I'll keep that in mind."

"This assignment can really draw you and Heather even more closely together if you consider her needs." Dennis said, "But I've also known couples that broke up during an international assignment."

"I get the message." Troy said, "It really is the Life's Pie thing on steroids."

"Yes." Dennis said, "Promise me, you'll stay aware of it."

"I definitely will." Troy answered, "And thank you for being such a great mentor and friend."

"I'm proud of you Troy." Dennis said, "You'll make a great international Executive Director."

Troy had barely hung up the phone when Cheryl Masters called.

"Well, Troy" Cheryl started, "Who would have guessed that two misfits like us would be international executive directors?"

"Hi Cheryl." Troy answered, "I'm excited but I have no idea what the job will actually entail."

"You know more than you think." Cheryl reassured Troy, "Remember a few months ago when you thought you couldn't assess people? You really caught on quickly. It will be the same in this assignment. Besides, you and I will work through a lot of it together."

"Yes." Troy answered, "And I'm grateful for that."

"Me too." Cheryl said, "Have you heard all the details about the buy-out?"

"No." Troy answered, "Fill me in."

"Well, it seems that your predecessor, Brian and three of his friends owned Redfern. The President wasn't an owner, but he was aware of the bribes to providers. He thought the money was being used for 'under the table' discounts. Redfern was shut down and Brian a got a two-year sentence in a white-collar prison and a huge fine. Our dear old president agreed to a plea bargain and got off with probation and community service. Scott Sedman was fired as were several reps." Cheryl said.

"Wow. I hadn't heard." Troy commented, "Scott was involved?"

"Yes." Cheryl answered, "Mostly involved with the gift cards part of the program. Can you believe it? And he was giving you a hard time about Redfern during the business plan presentation. He was part of it."

"Did the company have any repercussions?" Troy asked.

"McManus agreed to pay the federal government fines for Mareno's sins and that's how they became the white knight in the buy-out. McManus wanted nearly all the Mareno senior management out of the company. They couldn't find anything to pin on Sam, so they promoted him to President of EAA. Your old boss, Linh Ng got one of the two sales lead positions. The other went to one of the McManus people. They moved Jim Martin to accounting and Buzz agreed to take a District Manager's job. I think they're expecting Sam to fail and that he will be gone at the end of the 24 months, as well."

"They don't know Sam very well." Troy laughed, "We're going to find a way to succeed in international."

"My thoughts exactly." Cheryl said.

"Where are you going to manage Europe from?" Troy asked.

"Ever been to Barcelona?" Cheryl asked.

"Once." Troy said, "What a beautiful city."

"Well that's the new headquarters for Europe." Cheryl said, "And I understand that you're going to Hong Kong."

"Yes. I can't wait." Troy said. "In fact, Heather and going

for the first time on Monday."

"Any fears?" Cheryl asked.

"Tons." Troy answered honestly. "I'll be managing three country managers who know far more about their businesses than I do. And that only covers China, India and Australia. I have to hire country managers for 9 other countries."

"Same for me." Cheryl said, "I have country managers for the UK, France and Italy. The rest of Europe is wide open."

"What are you going to do?" Troy asked.

"The same as you." Cheryl answered, "Ask questions, learn from my direct reports, observe, try not to offend anyone right off the bat and hope that in time I can provide value."

"That sounds good, but won't they expect us to have the answers up front?" Troy asked.

"When you were new in the regional manager role did you ever talk to Greta in human resources? Cheryl asked.

"Sure." Troy said, "I asked her what to prepare when meeting my first team of direct reports.

"What did she tell you to do?" Cheryl asked.

"Funny you should ask." Troy said, "I was all worried about vision and expectations and she told me all they really wanted to know at the beginning was whether I was a good guy."

"You think people in Asia want to know the same thing?" Cheryl asked.

"Wow." Troy exclaimed, "Thank you so much. I had forgotten."

Troy hung up the phone with a greater sense of confidence that if he recaptured the many lessons of the past year from each of his mentors he could be as successful in Asia as he had quickly become in the United States.

The following Monday Troy and Heather boarded a wide-body jet in San Francisco heading to Hong Kong. They were as keyed up as children sitting in their business class pods that reclined fully to make a comfortable bed for the long 16-hour flight. Like many travelers flying to the west across many time zones they were amused by losing a day while crossing the international date line and realized that their lives were about to change as dramatically as that loss in time.

The morning sun reflected off the tall buildings rising against the mountainous backdrop of Hong Kong. The world was one of adventure and high energy with rushing cars, bikes and pedestrians coming and going from all directions. Heather and Troy tried not to look like tourists as they stood in awe of the unique sights and sounds of this vibrant Asian city. This would be the place of their greatest memories, the birthplace of their son, Blake and the place where Troy would establish his legacy of success.

These early thoughts would soon become happy memories. As time went by, there were many evenings when Troy would sit in front of his townhome in Mandalay Bay looking out at the China Sea wondering how all of this could have happened in such a short time; how someone with ordinary skills could come to lead others and be viewed as a success. Yet, here he was living a life that he couldn't have even imagined on that President's Cup trip when Sam gave him the break that changed his life.

QUESTIONS TO CONSIDER:

1) Troy took a risk for an international assignment; Buzz took a demotion to District Manager. What figured into both decisions and which would you most likely do?

2) Does your company offer cross-cultural training?

3) Does your company offer counseling for transitional depression?

4) What rules would you follow if put in a management position over those who have greater knowledge?

CHAPTER SEVENTEEN: A NEW BEGINNING

Many years had passed since those days at Mareno Biosciences. The international part of the business exceeded expectations. Sam retired four years after the buy-out. Cheryl Martin replaced Sam as President of McManus-Mareno Health International and later was appointed to the Board of Directors.

Linh led the Eastern Sales Division for three years before being promoted to Vice President of Sales in the United States.

Dennis retired from his corporate accounts position and started his own Life Coaching business teaching executives throughout the United States to better manage their own "Life's Pie".

Buzz survived the original buy-out and the subsequent purchase of the company by an even larger pharmaceutical giant. He retired on the coast of South Carolina where he spends his time fishing and playing golf.

Jim Martin thrived in the culture of McManus-Mareno

and was promoted to comptroller where he retired comfortably but refused a retirement party as a symbol of support for the cost-containment principles of executive leadership.

Alex built a career as a sales representative and district manager before starting his own data management company. His company went public a few years later. He retired on his 40th birthday and became president of a non-profit organization.

Troy after several years heading up Asia for McManus-Mareno was offered an international executive position for one of the largest pharmaceutical companies in the world. His career thrived as he held positions of increasing responsibility for all of Europe and Asia. He continued his education and achieved both an MBA and a PhD. He traveled over 100 days per year and despite significant efforts to coordinate travel with Heather and Blake often felt that he was sacrificing some areas of his "life's pie" for success at work.

Troy did make it home for Blake's fifteenth birthday, a celebration that was made special by Troy arranging for a visit to the intimate party by Blake's favorite professional soccer stars who also did commercials for Troy's company.

Blake's birthday seemed nearly perfect until the young man blew out the candles on the cake. When Troy asked Blake what he wished for he looked up and said, "I wish that you were here for more of my soccer games." It seemed to Troy that of all the lessons he had learned from mentors, the very first lesson Dennis tried to teach him so long ago was never fully realized. Troy never fully balanced his "Life's Pie".

Later that night, Troy sat in the library having a glass of

Bailey's Irish Crème when his cell phone began to buzz. Slightly irritated that he hadn't turned the phone off Troy picked it up and started to hit the red "reject call" button when he recognized the number. He immediately took the call.

"Sam?" Troy said, "It's been ages. How are you?"

"I'm fine Troy but I need you." Sam answered.

"Whatever you need." Troy answered, "What can I do for you?"

"How do you feel about San Diego?" Sam asked.

"San Diego?" Troy asked, "That's a great town. Why?"

"There's this school here. They call themselves a school of management" Sam said, "I've been serving as interim president."

"Well that's great Sam." Troy answered, "But what does that have to do with me?"

"I said I was an interim President." Sam said, "They need the real deal."

"What are you asking?" Troy said.

"I want you to give up your big corporate job and make a difference in people's lives by helping this school learn to teach tomorrow's managers." Sam said directly.

"I would be giving up a lot." Troy said

"I get that. But I think you might gain a bit as well." Sam said. Then after a brief silence Sam continued. "Let me ask you something. Do you trust me?"

"Of course, I trust you." Troy answered with a smile, remembering the same conversation so many years ago.

"Then trust me with your career." Sam said

"I always have, Sam." Troy said, "I always have."

The STAR Manager

The deep blue Pacific Ocean could be seen in the distance through the windows of a lecture hall in San Diego where 135 students of executive management anxiously took notes as the new president of the college began his lecture

"I have a task for you this morning. Write down the name of every manager you ever worked for." The President ordered.

The students quickly wrote names on blank pieces of paper. As the rustling of pen and paper came to a halt the President continued.

"How many names on your list?"

The professor tallied the numbers on the white board at the front of the lecture hall.

"Now, go back to your list and place a star next to the name of any manager that made a fundamental difference in your life."

The students marked their lists and the professor noted the vastly reduced number of managers with stars as compared to the totals listed on the white boards.

"Ladies and gentlemen, how is it possible that so many managers tried to make a difference yet failed so miserably? The reason you are here is to become that manager who has a star next to their name for every single person you are blessed to manage in the future. For success is not measured in salaries and titles but rather in the number of lives that you have enhanced throughout your careers. Management, my friends is a calling. There are many who will be bosses but it is my hope...my fervent desire...my greatest prayer... that each of you will not just be a manager but rather will be a STAR manager."

Troy passed out the syllabus of the management course and as he reviewed it with the class felt a flood of memories of those early days as southeast regional manager at Mareno Biosciences.

Troy looked at each topic and thought of those who had influenced his success in management. He suddenly thought of Dennis, Cheryl, Jim, Buzz, Scott, Greta, Alex and of course, Sam.

The syllabus was a review of so many lessons provided to Troy by his mentors. The Executive Management Course Included:

Introduction to Management	"A tough day" "judgement and experience" "Life's Pie" "Integrity, Trust and Respect"
Business Planning	"Hope is not a strategy" "Determining What's Possible" "Managers don't think, they know" "Determining Sales and Unit Goals" "Structure of Business Planning" "The test of Sufficiency" "The test of the Non-essential"
Vision/Mission of the Team	"Competition should be external, not internal" "7 Expectations" "Identifying the Non-negotiables" Personal Integrity is the "North Star"
Recruiting and Selection	"Methods of Ongoing Recruiting" "Use of Competency models" "Selection Standards" "Five Points of Contact"

	"Balancing Team Diversity"
	"Halo effect"
Coaching	"CARE Coaching methodology"
	"Determining the right WHAT"
	"Identifying consequences WHY"
	"Planning for success HOW"
	"Timeline and Follow up WHEN"
Assessing Talent	"Major Areas of Competency"
	"Using the quick assessment"
	"Documentation and Input"
	"Consistency"
Work Session Planning	"If you can name it and understand it you can change it"
	"The most important business issue"
	"The most important skill issue"
Management Style	"What is your style?"
	"Adapting management style to others"
	"The Managerial Toolbox"
Special Issues of Executive Leadership	"Relocation Planning"
	"Cross-cultural Planning"
	"Transitional Depression"
Managerial Ethics	Case Study

After asking a few questions about the syllabus the students filed out of the lecture hall enthusiastically discussing what they would be learning. One person remained still sitting in the now empty hall.

He slowly stood up, his gait unsure but his appearance crisp. His silver hair reflected the light of the sun shining through the window of the lecture hall.

He went up to the white board and picked up a marker.

He wrote the following:

Linh
Dennis
Cheryl
Jim
Buzz

And then in big letters **TROY NOBLE**

Then Sam placed stars next to each name, then turned to Troy and smiled.

Troy took the marker from Sam's frail hand and wrote in even bigger letters:

SAM LOGAN, adding a star of its own.

Troy looked at each of the names. He thought briefly of the strengths and the weaknesses of each. Linh with her straight-forward approach to people development and unassuming manner. Cheryl with her great read on people and her sometimes brash style. Jim with his amazing aptitude for business but his lack of self-awareness. Buzz, with his friendly but unpolished demeanor. Dennis with his excellent insights into the needs of others yet difficulty in dealing with stress. And Sam, a man who had the vision to lead a company to great success while looking through a clouded, dated cultural lens. Yet, every one of these managers had somehow made a fundamental difference in his life. Each one was truly a STAR manager to Troy.

Troy wondered how through leveraging strengths and minimizing weaknesses each could have been STAR managers to far more people. Troy further wondered how many of his direct reports over the years would have placed a star next to his name.

Sam and Troy shook hands, paused and then embraced each other in a giant bear hug.

I'm proud of you Troy." Sam said quietly, "You have made a difference in my life and in many others, as well. Take care of these bright young students and the instructors that will mold them. Make sure they learn what it's all about. Teach them to be STAR Managers."

"After having you as my mentor." Troy said, "If I can't do that then I should be arrested for impersonating a…"

Sam rolled his eyes and turned away waving his hand behind him. "Yeah, yeah, yeah…" he mumbled as he walked away.

THE END

ABOUT THE AUTHOR

Don Cope is a sales, marketing, training and development professional whose company, Shinestar Consulting Services provides managerial training and professional development for medical device and pharmaceutical companies both in the United States and internationally. Don "retired" after 31 years as an executive of the largest healthcare corporation in the world.

Don lives with the philosophy that there are few true barriers that can limit our horizons. As a result, since his initial retirement he has enjoyed sky-diving, zip-lining through the rain forest, helicoptering to the top of a glacier, dog-sledding across the frozen tundra and rafting through a jungle. He also has learned to compete in ballroom dancing and most importantly fell in love again and was recently married to his friend and business partner, Wendy Wood, LMHC.

As a new author, Don has written The Nephilim Factor and The STAR Manager.

Don lives in downtown St. Petersburg, Florida, a place he often calls "Little Paradise".

For information regarding speaking engagements and training workshops please contact Don at shinestardrc@verizon.net or visit the shinestar webpage at www.shinestarconsulting.net

While driving across a bridge in a driving rainstorm, Joe sees a car in the water quickly sinking into the lake. Hearing cries for help, he jumps in the water to save a mother and her two children. During the heroic rescue Joe gets disoriented in the murky lake and is transported to another world, a novel place where he is exposed to planets he's never heard of and encounters experiences that shatter his understanding of all things spiritual.

In this new world, Joe encounters a guide who helps him to understand life's greatest mysteries, including the question that has always haunted Joe the most; what causes extreme evil on earth?

Joe learns the incredible story of angels who were granted free will and came to earth, impregnated human woman and whose offspring changed the very course of history. These amazing creatures were called The Nephilim.

People throughout the world know the story of creation in the book of Genesis yet have overlooked the strange verse just a few chapters later. "The Nephilim were on the earth in those days--and also afterward--when the sons of God went to the daughters of humans and had children by them. They were the heroes of old, men of renown."

Who were these creatures and how could they still impact our world today? The shocking conclusion of The Nephilim Factor provides a chilling explanation of how evil might be living right next door!

Donald Cope

www.ingramcontent.com/pod-product-compliance
Lightning Source LLC
Chambersburg PA
CBHW050200230526
45470CB00001B/168